Bipolar Disorder

Step by Step Techniques to Manage Bipolar Disorder

(Living With Bipolar Disorder Patient & Managing Bipolar Disorder)

Patrick Dotson

Published By **Bengion Cosalas**

Patrick Dotson

All Rights Reserved

Bipolar Disorder: Step by Step Techniques to Manage Bipolar Disorder (Living With Bipolar Disorder Patient & Managing Bipolar Disorder)

ISBN 978-1-7752672-4-9

No part of this guidebook shall be reproduced in any form without permission in writing from the publisher except in the case of brief quotations embodied in critical articles or reviews.

Legal & Disclaimer

The information contained in this ebook is not designed to replace or take the place of any form of medicine or professional medical advice. The information in this ebook has been provided for educational & entertainment purposes only.

The information contained in this book has been compiled from sources deemed reliable, and it is accurate to the best of the Author's knowledge; however, the Author cannot guarantee its accuracy and validity and cannot be held liable for any errors or omissions. Changes are periodically made to this book. You must consult your doctor or get professional medical advice before using any of the suggested remedies, techniques, or information in this book.

Upon using the information contained in this book, you agree to hold harmless the Author from and against any damages, costs, and expenses, including any legal fees potentially resulting from the application of any of the information provided by this guide. This disclaimer applies to any damages or injury caused by the use and application, whether directly or indirectly, of any advice or information presented, whether for breach of contract, tort, negligence, personal injury, criminal intent, or under any other cause of action.

You agree to accept all risks of using the information presented inside this book. You need to consult a professional medical practitioner in order to ensure you are both able and healthy enough to participate in this program.

Table Of Contents

Chapter 1: Understanding Borderline

Personality Disorder

What exactly is a "borderline personality disorder"?

Borderline personality disorder (BPD), which can be described as a high-stress state, will make it seem like you're constantly on the move. You might feel lost or confused in terms of your self-image, goals, and even likes/dislikes.

BPD sufferers often feel too sensitive. Some liken it the feeling of having one nerve ending exposed. You may get strong reactions to small things. It's hard to find peace once you're upset. It's easy enough to see that emotional instability or inability of self-soothe can lead impulsive, even reckless behavior and relationship problems. It's difficult for people to remain calm and focused when they are overwhelmed by emotion. You may say or perform in a dangerous or unprofessional manner. This could leave you feeling embarrassed or guilty. It can become a vicious cycle that can seem unbreakable.

But it isn't. BPD therapy and coping strategies may help you feel better.
BPD can usually be treated.
Many mental healthcare professionals concluded that BPD was not treatable. We now know that BPD may be managed. BPD offers a better long term prognosis than either depression or bipolar illnesses. It does however require a specific treatment. The important thing to remember is that BPD sufferers can and do recover. And they do so quickly with the right therapies and support.

Healing is the process of breaking destructive patterns in thought, behavior, and feeling that are causing pain. It is not easy to get rid of lifelong habits. It may feel awkward and strange at first to stop and reflect before acting. Over time, you will develop new habits that will help keep you in control and your emotional balance.

Treatment of borderline personality disorder.
Are you willing to agree with any one of the following statements
I often feel "empty."

My emotions change rapidly and I often feel extreme grief, rage, or worry.
I'm always afraid that those I love will abandon or leave me.

My most intense love relationships were unstable and often difficult.
My feelings toward people in my family can shift dramatically from one minute to the next. I'm not sure why.

I frequently engage with risky or hazardous behaviors such as driving recklessly, having unsafe sex, binging on alcohol, taking drugs, and going on spending binges.

I have tried to inflict harm on myself, used self-harm such as cutting, and even threatened to commit suicide.
I can become irritable in relationships and lash out, or make rash gestures just to keep the other person near.

If you identify with some of the statements above, you might have borderline personality syndrome.
BPD can be mistakenly misdiagnosed with other conditions. Even if a diagnosis is not made, self-help tips in this book could be helpful in relieving your emotional distress and helping you manage your self-destructive tendencies.
Signs and symptoms

Borderline personality disorders (BPD) can manifest in many different ways. But, for diagnostic purposes, mental health experts classify the symptoms within nine basic categories. BPD is diagnosed when you have at least five signs. BPD must also be chronic, meaning they often begin in puberty and can affect many areas of your lives. BPD symptoms: 9

Fear of being forgotten: People with BPD have a tendency to be afraid of being neglected or abandoned. Even seemingly insignificant events, such a loved-one returning home late at night or leaving on the weekend, can trigger deep anxiety. This could result in panicked attempts at keeping the other person nearby. You might plead for, cling, create conflicts, follow your loved-one's whereabouts, stop them from fleeing or even physically hinder them from doing so. Unfortunately, your behavior could have the opposite result of repelling others.

BPD patients are known for having unstable relationships. These relationships can be passionate and brief-lasting. You might quickly fall in and out of love, hoping each new person would bring you joy, but then you'll be disappointed. Your relationships can be either fantastic or awful, with no in between. Your rapid swings of idealization to hatred, devaluation, wrath or anger can cause emotional whiplash in your family, friends, and lovers.

BPD often causes uncertainty or changes in self-image. Sometimes you are happy with yourself. Other times, you may hate yourself or consider yourself to be wicked. Most likely, you have no idea who you are and what you want. You might change your job, friends and relationships frequently.

BPD: Self-destructive, impulseive behavior: You may be impulsive or impulsive when you're distressed. You may spend money that isn't possible to afford, shoplift and indulge in unsanitary sex. These dangerous activities can temporarily improve your mood, but they are detrimental for you and others in the long term.

BPD is characterized by self-harm. Suicidal thoughts, suicidal acts or threats, aswell as suicide attempts, are all examples of suicidal behaviour. Self-harm is any attempt or effort to do harm to oneself that isn't suicidal. There are two main types of self harm: burning and cutting.

Extreme emotional ups or downs are associated with BPD. Sometimes you can be happy and sometimes depressed at the same time. Even small things, which others might overlook, can lead to an emotional spiral. These mood fluctuations, which can be powerful, usually vanish quickly.

Persistent feelings o emptiness: BPD sufferers often feel empty. At its extreme, it may feel like "nothing", or "nobody". You might feel the urge to fill the void with drugs, food, or sexual activity, as this is a very unpleasant feeling. Anger that explodes feels like nothing.

Feelings of extreme anger or a rapid temper: When the fuse is lit, you might have trouble controlling your anger, shouting, throwing things, or being overwhelmed by wrath. It's important to note that this rage does not always target others. You might spend a lot on yourself.

Feeling skeptical or disconnected from reality: BPD patients often experience paranoia. A condition known as dissociation, occurs when you become stressed and lose touch of reality. It is possible to feel disoriented, confused, or out-of-place.

Borderline personality disorder can often co-occur with disorders that are not easily diagnosed. Symptoms that are frequently co-occur with Borderline personality disorder include depression, bipolar disorder, eating disorders due to drug abuse, anxiety problems. If BPD is treated correctly, many other illnesses will improve. Sometimes, however, this is not true. For instance, you might be able to manage symptoms of depression and still struggle with BPD.

Causes of Borderline personality Disorder

Mental health specialists believe that borderline personality disease (BPD), which is also known as borderline personality disorder, can be caused by a combination or inheritance of biological and environmental characteristics. Brain differences Complex processes are taking place in the BPD brain. Experts still don't know what to make of it.

BPD is a condition where your brain is constantly on high alert. Things are often more stressful and frightening to you than they can be to others. The fight or flight response is quickly activated. Once activated it hijacks the logic brain and triggers survival instincts not appropriate for the situation.

Your brain is different than everyone else's. What are you going to do about it? You may be able to alter your mind. Every time that you apply a new coping method or self-soothing approach, new brain connections are created.

Some treatments, such mindfulness meditation, have the potential to increase your brain matter. These paths will become stronger as you continue to practice. Keep going! With time and effort, it is possible to change the way you think and feel.

When psychologists discuss personality disorders and stigmatization, they are referring the patterns of thinking and feeling that make us unique. We all act differently, but we can have relatively constant interactions and engagements in the environment. People are often described as "shy,"" outgoing," "meticulous,","fun-loving," etc. These are aspects or aspects of one's personality. A personality disorder is not an assessment of your character. "Personality disorder" can be described as a way to connect with an environment that is significantly different from the normal. (In other words: You don't behave the way most people expect. This results in constant trouble in many areas of your life: your relationships, career, thoughts, and how you view yourself and others. These designs can be changed, and that is the most important thing!

BPD (borderline personality disorders) has been a controversial diagnose since its inclusion into the Diagnostic and Statistical Manual of Mental Disorders of 1980. BPD is often confused with bipolar illness. However, they share many symptoms.

Chapter 2: The Difference Between

Bipolar Disorders And Borderline

Personality Disorder

Bipolar disease and BPD are thought to be connected by some experts because they share the trait of mood instability. Bipolar disorder causes mood swings that range from sadness to depression to mania. These mood fluctuations can also be accompanied by a decrease in sleep or an increase of activity.

BPD may also be associated with mood swings, which can sometimes be called emotional dysregulation. BPD is a condition where people can go from feeling perfectly fine to extremely disturbed in as little as a few minutes. Both people with bipolar disease as well as those with BPD are susceptible to impulsive behavior.

BPD: Reality

What's the difference between Bipolar Disorders and Borderline Personality Disorders (BID)?

What is the difference? There are many important differences between the two.

Both disorders can lead to mood changes. However the severity of these mood alterations will vary. Bipolar illness manifests as depression and manic episodes, while BPD causes deep emotional suffering. It is characterized in mania and depression.

Time: BPD mood swings may be temporary. These mood swings can last for only a few moments. Bipolar illness may cause mood swings which can last up to a few hours.

Cause: Mood swings with bipolar disorder are usually caused by an external stressor like a fight with a loved. But, mood shifts with BPD can happen unexpectedly.

Degree: BPD's mood swings don't often include joy. This transition occurs between feeling normal and feeling unhappy. It's not like feeling terrible to feel high or elevated as is typical for bipolar illness.

Is there a correlation between bipolar disorders and borderline personality disorders?

Although research isn't conclusive, it has been shown that there is no significant association between BPD and bipolar disorder. BPD patients are more likely that they will be diagnosed with bipolar disorder than people with other personality disorders.

One research found that approximately 20% of BPD patients have bipolar illness. Bipolar illness affects only around 10% of people with personality disorders.

Another research looked at patients diagnosed with both BPD or bipolar illness over a 10-year period. It was found that both conditions are completely distinct. The authors of the study stressed that each illness must be treated individually to achieve maximum improvement in symptoms.

Although there are some similarities, there isn't enough evidence to link BPD and Bipolar Disorder. There are similarities but also differences between BPD & bipolar disorder.

BPD and bipolar disorders can co-occur, but it is not sufficient to prove their connection. It is important to continue research in this area. Future researches, for instance, on the molecular and genetic underpinnings BPD and bipolar disease, may reveal previously unknown relationships between the two conditions.

Borderline Personality Triggers

The term "trigger" has many negative implications. I almost always substitute the word "catalyst," when dealing with clients or their families, with "triggers". BPD behavior is defined as the catalyst, which refers to events or actions that lead to problematic thoughts, emotions and behaviors.

Here's an example.

Kate is a sensitive, 19-year old girl who is now attending college for her freshman years. She has several housemates whom she met on her first day in college. Kate, like most freshmen in college, is eager make friends and be accepted. She is also afraid about being rejected.

In the first few weeks, Kate's roommate makes a decision not to like Kate. She acts politely yet coolly towards Kate.

Kate is filled by shame, regret, anger, and remorse following her rejection. "There's some problem with me," she thought. Kate calls her mom in tears less a week after her graduation, telling her that no one at college liked her and that her desire to go home is strong.

This scenario is why students want to quit school because of the apparent rejection. The ideas and emotions surrounding this incident cause the behavior.

Recognizing the triggers that can lead to BPD symptoms is a crucial step in your recovery.

It is important to recognize that every person has their own triggers. There is no "one-size fits all" solution. However, certain catalysts tend to be more prevalent than others. Here are some examples:

The feeling of abandonment

Hurting another's feelings
Rejection from any source (even strangers)

The dissolution of a significant relationship
Resigning or being fired from a job
A Memoir of a Horror Incident
Although there may be many causes of extreme emotion dysregulation, most people feel the most vulnerable to fear of rejection, abandonment, and exclusion. If a person feels abandoned, ignored or mistreated, they are likely to be emotional. Anger can also stem from the fact that someone has been rejected or deserted. Also, people may feel rejected and invalidated. It can also lead to self-destructive behaviours, drug misuse, selfharm and suicide.

Worst of all, a catalyst might not be considered a major event in the eyes of someone with BPD. Below is a list that

includes seemingly benign triggers that may lead people to develop BPD.
No callback when asked
A party invitation is not sent
Refusal to answer basic questions

It is not possible to be called upon in class
Exclusion from a decisionmaking process

Being ignored, chastised or judged
People may feel ignored if they have the perception that they aren't being heard. This can cause them to engage in behaviors that are not consistent or aligned with their goals and beliefs. Recognizing trends can help you deal with your problems more effectively.
Can or should you eliminate "triggers?"
It is very unlikely that all potential triggers and/or catalysts for unproductive behaviors can be identified and eliminated. As difficult as

life can be, we don't need to protect our loved ones from the effects of distressing situations. Some people believe that tough situations help them to grow and increase their emotional resilience. (I also believe this!)

It's a nice (and kind!) thing to help someone cope with traumatic events. BPD sufferers will be able to learn how to calm down and what their problematic ways of problem solving are.

Chapter 3: How Bpd Affects

Relationships

Relationships & borderline personality disorder

BPD patients have problems with platonic and romantic relationships. BPD sufferers and partners with BPD have particular issues when it comes to romantic relations.

BPD symptoms can cause severe emotional swings.

BPD patients may feel loving and tender, but they could experience a shift in their emotions within a matter hours. They might feel overwhelmed or suffocated. They might decide to move on from the partner that they are trying to be closer to.

BPD patients may be able to build healthy relationships through therapy and continued support from their loved ones and partners. Continue reading for more information about BPD and what you can to do if you or a spouse have it. What is the definition and treatment of borderline personality disorders?

Borderline personality disorder, also known as BPD, is a mental condition that affects the way people feel about ordinary emotions.

BPD patients tend to be impulsive as well as emotionally unstable. You may feel agitated, anxious, or sad. These outbursts could last several hours before being followed by more stability. These episodes can be severe and last for several days. They can also have an adverse effect on relationships, work, and personal health. BPD patients are more likely than others to harm themselves, cause accidents, or engage in conflict. BPD sufferers are more likely than others to commit suicide.

An alternative approach to understanding the views of someone with BPD, is to recognize how difficult they find it to return to a normal emotional state.

An individual may feel more joy if something is enjoyable or exciting. This can last for a greater amount of time. The opposite can be true as well: individuals may feel more joy if something unpleasant happens.

These emotional peaks, lows, and highs can be confusing to loved ones and partners, which can lead to intense and conflict-filled interactions.

What if you're in an intimate relationship with someone who has BPD.

BPD can make romantic relationships difficult. It's not uncommon for there to be significant turbulence.

BPD sufferers on the other side can be very kind, sensitive, and affectionate. Some people appreciate this level in a relationship. BPD sufferers might also be extremely physically active, anxious to spend as many time with their spouse.

BPD sufferers also have a sensitive reaction to abandonment and rejection. Many people are worried about what signals may indicate that a lover is unhappy or leaving them.

BPD sufferers who notice changes in their partner's emotions, real or imagined, may immediately retreat. BPD may make them angry or feel hurt by something that someone else would not. They may also develop compulsive and paranoid tendencies.

These emotional ups & downs can sometimes be hard to handle. They can sometimes lead to awkward situations in public. BPD patients may become impulsive, which can lead to a breakdown in their relationship.

A stable relationship can, however, have a beneficial influence on BPD patients' emotional sensitivity. BPD sufferers can form long-term marriages or relationships that last for many years with little effort on their part.

How can BPD affect your relationships? BPD symptoms can harm relationships. If you have been diagnosed with this illness, you may be aware. BPD patients are more likely have multiple romantic relationships.

This could be because your partner ended the relationship. This could have been because you were afraid that the other person would do the opposite. It could be that your partner was not comfortable dealing with such adversity.

It is vital to understand that, regardless of your personality type, you could still have a loving relationship. Together with a solid support system, treatment can help to achieve emotional and interpersonal stability.

BPD is not curable. However, treatment will help you to manage your symptoms.

BPD Management
These are the most commonly used treatments for BPD.
Therapy. BPD sufferers frequently benefit from dialytic behavioral

therapy. The therapist will show how to deal with emotions with logic and discretion. This will reduce the dualistic thinking (the idea that everything is either white or black) that so many people with BPD are prone to.

Medication. BPD can not be treated with pharmaceuticals. However, certain symptoms may be helped by antidepressants or antianxiety drugs and antipsychotics.

Hospitalization. Your doctor may recommend hospitalization if you are exhibiting signs of suicidal or self-harm.
If one of you has bipolar disorder, making a relationship work is not possible

BPD can affect both you and your spouse. It is possible to learn to manage the emotional cycle that the disorder creates. This can help to create a stronger, more resilient partnership.

Methods to Improve BPD Relationships

Learn more information about BPD. Understanding what your spouse is going through with BPD is an important part of caring. You can understand their emotional state and how you can help them to cope.

Seek expert assistance. BPD sufferers with a diagnosis can be helped by therapy. This will help them to cope with their emotions and overcome any negative experiences. BPD-related partners may benefit from therapy. Partner can benefit from professional support in understanding, understanding and being supportive.

Provide emotional assistance. People with BPD may feel isolated because of their past. Give your partner patience.

It is possible for them both to learn and behave more well.

Relationship opportunities

BPD can lead to healthy relationships because they have a tendency to be kind and understanding. It takes effort. There will always be obstacles.

In order to help you or your partner, doctors and therapists can work together. These healthcare experts can help you deal with the BPD symptoms which are most detrimental to your relationship.

How to care for someone with BPD patiently

To care for someone suffering from borderline personality disorder requires patience, effective communication skills as well as firm limits and an open mind to learning more about the disease. The treatment of borderline personality disorder may be effective in relieving symptoms. However, it can take time. Family members must learn about BPD and the treatment options. They also need to be patient with their loved ones who are determined to get better. What is it like to have Borderline personality Disorder?

To help someone suffering from borderline personality disorder. Start by researching the signs and symptoms of borderline personality disorders so you can help your family member. This will enable you to be more patient with your loved ones in distress and show empathy. If you don't know what the condition is, it can be hard to sympathize. The person appears manipulative, needy, illogical, as well as not working hard enough for their health. It is quite different from the inside.

There are some common misconceptions about BPD. It is important to be aware of these in order to help you better understand what the sufferers go through and how they feel. BPD sufferers do not try to manipulate or be manipulative. Instead, they fear being left behind. They aren't selfish people. Although they care deeply for their loved ones, it is hard for them to show selfishness when they are also experiencing their own emotions. They desire to change but it is very difficult.

These are some instances of BPD that you might feel.

Being aware of other people's actions and words

You feel powerful emotions, like you are riding a rollercoaster.

Fear of losing your loved one is something you should be constantly afraid of, even if that seems unlikely.

In urgent need for reassurance

Feeling inferior and rejected

Feelings such as terror, sadness, anguish, and anger that you're unable or unwilling to handle

Feeling unimportant, empty, or unable to identify oneself.

Signs someone could have BPD

What is borderline personality syndrome? It is a form personality disorder. This mental illness causes an individual to have trouble controlling their thoughts, feelings, behavior, and thoughts. A normal life can be made difficult by the presence of intense emotions, shifting moods or fear of abandonment, self harm, unstable relationships, an inability to control your anger, paranoias, rage and violence, as well as other symptoms.

Here are some indicators that you suspect the subject of your concern has BPD.

Your loved one's moods change quickly, often in just minutes.

It is almost like you walk on eggshells. The loved one you love is experiencing severe sadness or an anxiety attack.

Everything is on your shoulders, and your loved-one criticizes you because you don't understand.

A friend or family member has tried to commit suicide, by cutting or burning themselves.

You may suspect your loved is manipulating.

Your loved ones think you're extraordinary one moment, and awful the following.

Your loved one is likely to change employment, activities and hobbies.

You are often concerned about your loved person's unsafe activities.

Diagnosis and Treatment of Borderline Personality Disorder

If you are concerned about someone you love and see signs of borderline personality disorder, it is a good idea to seek professional help. This can be a challenging phase as the borderline personality traits may be more evident on the exterior. You may not see any change in the way someone is thinking or acting. It is vital to convince your loved-one to visit a doctor.

Although borderline personality testing is not possible, a thorough interview, physical exam, and mental examination can help a mental specialist make an accurate diagnosis. There are several criteria for borderline personality disorders. If your loved ones meets at least five, they will most likely be diagnosed. While you can speak with any physician, it is best to have your loved one diagnosed by a psychiatrist. He or she can then refer you for any necessary drugs and can confirm the diagnosis.

BPD Treatment Support and Management

After getting a diagnosis, your loved can start to work on a plan of treatment for borderline personality disorder. While there is no treatment for borderline personality disorders, your loved-one may be offered medication for anxiety, sadness, or other psychotic symptoms. Your loved one should follow the instructions and never skip any medication. You should keep a list of adverse effects and report them to your doctor.

Dialectical behaviour therapy (DBT), a component of BPD management, teaches patients to become more aware and tolerant towards their emotions, bad thinking and moods. Students are taught how to manage their emotions and prevent them from committing any untoward actions. Studies show that this kind of therapy as well as family psychological education have the best results for those suffering from BPD. Family psychoeducation is an educational program that helps family members understand bipolar disorder and help patients. Get suggestions from your doctor about a program you could participate in.

Do you need effective BPD treatments?
Communication Tips
Relationships are one the most challenging aspects for borderline

personality disorder. Learn how to be with your loved one.

Your loved one deserves your attention. He or she should know that your attention is paid and that you value their opinions. First listen and then answer to show that they heard you.

Don't try and convince your loved-one that you are right, or that you have the upper hand. It won't work.

It is important to remember that it is not a good idea to take in negative comments personally. Be open to hearing the emotions and not the hurtful words.

Talk to your loved ones gently no matter how outof control they are. If you're unable to keep your cool and are not able to communicate well, it is best to move on.

You can distract your loved one from emotions that are getting out of control. Try music, TV, an art project, exercise, and anything else to distract you.

Limits

While caring for someone suffering from a borderline personality disorder it is vital to set and enforce boundaries. This will not only make it easier for you to care for your loved one, but will also help teach them how to respect boundaries and communicate with others. The consequences of crossing the boundaries should be made clear.

The boundary that you can create is that you won't allow your loved one to call each other derogatory names when you are having an emotional reaction or arguing. While it may be helpful for your loved one to shout, name-calling does not allow. Tell your loved one to stop using abusive language and tell them that it will end the conversation. Boundaries shouldn't be harsh but fair. Don't put your loved-one in danger.

Suicidal Behaviors & Self-Harm

BPD patients are not likely to want to die. However their strong emotions, as well guilt and shame can lead to self harm and suicide. These are not something to be taken lightly. Self-harm (such a cutting and burning) is not usually suicidal. But it can provide relief for emotional problems. Your loved one and the therapist can discuss alternate ways to get relief.

Though suicide threats and other acts should be taken seriously. Your response could actually be strengthening. Be straight-forward and not emotional, and avoid coddling or giving attention and affection that isn't necessary. Tell your loved ones not to do that, ask for information, validate the emotions, and seek assistance if necessary. If necessary, dial 911.

Support for the BPD caregiver
Caregiving for someone with a borderline personality condition is important. This is an emotionally unstable personality disorder and it can be difficult to live with or love someone with it. If you are not taking care of yourself, your loved one will be unable help them as fully as possible. Here are some essential self-care practices:
You can help. Not only is your loved one in need of assistance, but you too. Keep in touch with family and friends. They will listen to you and support your needs. The support group can be very helpful for those with personality disorders.

It is important to make time for yourself. Even though it takes a lot to care for someone who has BPD, you still deserve to live your life. It is okay to take a break from caring for someone with BPD. Instead, do something that you are passionate about.

Take control of your tension. This tough connection can cause tension. Learn stress relief and coping techniques to reduce it. All forms of meditation, including yoga, mindfulness practice and breathing techniques, are beneficial.

Take care of you. You may lose focus on your health because of other priorities. This is not acceptable. Good physical health is key to a good life. You will be able to deal better if you get enough sleep, exercise and eat right. It's well worth the effort.

Keep in mind, this is not your fault. It's easy, all too easily, to get caught in a cycle blame, guilt and responsibility that isn't yours. This is not your fault. Only love and support can be given.

The experience of living with borderline personality disorder (BPD) can be challenging for both the patient and their loved ones. You can support this individual's therapy and help him or her to learn to communicate clearly, establish boundaries, as well as take care to yourself. BPD therapy will take time to show results. Be patient. Your loved one's recovery will be made easier by your continued support.

Chapter 4: Communicating With

Someone Suffering From Bpd

Borderline Personality Disorder (BPD), one of the most distressing aspects, can make it difficult for people with it to communicate well. We respond to our triggers frequently by framing our statements so that they appear to worsen the situation.

Sometimes, it can seem like all your options are exhausted. There have been many things you tried, such as giving up, denying facts, or trying to avoid the situation. Even if there are good intentions and you make great efforts to resolve conflicts between Borderline Personality Disorder patients, it can be hard for people to know how they should approach the conversation.

You can improve your communication skills with Borderline Personality Condition-related people, friends, family members, and coworkers. BPD therapy is taught by mental health professionals. These techniques can help to decrease the severity and frequency in high-conflict discussions. All that's required is a desire and ability to practice.

Here are some suggestions for better communication with someone with Borderline Personality Syndrome:

Validation must be provided.

Many Borderline Personality disorders sufferers were raised with parents who disregarded their feelings, wishes, or worries. BPD can cause people to appear unlogical. They may react in an illogical way to perceived slights or misunderstand others' intentions.

It's very easy to respond to them with comments like, "That's crazy." "I'm not sure why you feel that way. I asked you a simple question." This statement may seem to be a rational answer to the person suffering from BPD. But it effectively discredits the person's feelings, and increases their emotions.

Validation can be a game changer. Let's say, "Let you explain." Do you think you do a poor job when you ask me about your employment? That could be why it might bother you. We don't condone any bad behavior or wrath. However, by simply acknowledging how the person suffering from BPD feels, we convey that we are listening rather than judging.

Other Communication Strategies Available for People with BPD

Borderline Personality Disorder sufferers will be more open to problem solving if they feel heard and understood. Some other ways you can improve communication with your BPD loved person include:

Listen. Pay attention when your loved one speaks. To demonstrate you have heard your loved one, ask questions. Then repeat what they said. Avoid distractions and make sure you have enough time to converse.

Take your time. Don't let frustration get in the way. Accept the fact communication may be difficult for your BPD friend. It may take some time for them and you to feel comfortable talking with one another.

Before you respond, consider all your options. Instead of reacting immediately to what your loved-one has said, take time to evaluate your response. This can help you come up with a better answer that moves the conversation forward, and not stifles it.

BPD Lovers

BPD (Borderline Personity Disorder) can be difficult to love. There are both risks and rewards. BPD symptoms, such as mood swings that are severe, fear of abandonment and emotional reactivity, can make it difficult to live a happy, peaceful life.

If your loved one is struggling with complex childhood traumas and Complex PTSD, you will probably see the world differently. It's helpful to learn about their environment to understand their behavior.

Love someone with Borderline Personality Syndrome takes courage, patience, and a lot of faith. There are certain circumstances that could lead to you being hurt. For example, your loved one might make false accusations, be furious at others, or blames other people for their behavior. This can be difficult and stressful without the right support. Sometimes it is difficult to see or recall that their behavior is not directed at you. It comes from their issues.

Here are some examples illustrating psychological phenomena that might be occurring in people.

'TOO REASONABLE' Emotions

Psychologists call this 'psychic equality'. A mental state in the which they can't distinguish between their feelings and thoughts and the outside world. Your loved ones may misunderstand their feelings, thoughts and beliefs as objective facts. Fear, anxiety or contempt for someone they don't like are all reality to them. When they feel criticized, they believe they are being critiqued. The feelings of self-criticism and humiliation can become so overwhelming that they can even be harmful. BPD love means your loved one doesn't always see the same things as you. They can withdraw into a regressive state if they are injured, making it more difficult to get in touch with them. It is possible to feel annoyed and lonely when this happens.

A BPD lover will know that OUTSIGHT IS OUTOF MIND.

This is known in psychology as a lack or object constancy. In order to relate to others, it may be difficult for your loved ones to maintain a consistent mental picture. They may have trouble maintaining consistency and continuity within their relationships. Imagine playing peekaboo, with a youngster. When you take a toy out, it seems like it has vanished. Your BPD-loving friend will also find this true: When they don't see your face, it's almost like you don't even exist.

BPD sufferers experience extreme anxiety when other people leave. The intense desire to keep their self-sense intact without the help of someone else can cause BPD severe anxiety.

BPD patients need to feel loved and supported by someone. You might feel compelled by your feelings to keep reminding them about your love and concern. If you don't, others will think you have lost touch with them. Individuals find it difficult to maintain a feeling of 'loving presence' without regular reminders. This could appear as clinging, jealous behavior.

RAGE AND EXTREME SIGNIFICATION

Your behavior could be understood by others as if there were no context. Instead, you may interpret your actions and intentions based on how they have been interacted with. You might think that everything you say provokes a fury or that you are always misunderstood. You may also find them sensitive to criticism.

You should not try to judge the emotions of someone with BPD. You might be very aware of the emotions and intentions of your loved ones. It is possible for them to detect your emotions or intentions before you even realize. Recognizing your role can help to ease the wrath.

If you love someone with BPD, you should not approach them with the condition. However, you can talk to your loved one about your worries, offer information connections, and inform them that they have access to successful therapies when they're ready.

BPD Lovers: How to deal With Tensions

BPD comes with many advantages. These benefits are often not mentioned because many BPD patients feel that they are on the fringes of society. BPD can bring out the best in people. However, when you spend time with them, it's easy to feel as if you don't really know who you will get. It's difficult to love someone suffering from BPD.

BPD can be a dangerous combination. It is not necessary to break up with your partner. Here are some tips to help you get through heated arguments.

Be as attentive as possible.

BPD sufferers are highly sensitive to signs of abandonment and rejection. (Object Permanence is a theory that explains why this is true. Even if the goal is to stay, people can feel disconnected or shut off. They are very intuitive and attentive. If you simply say yes to something without listening, they will feel it.

It is hard to stay awake at all times when you're dealing with someone intensely fast-paced. They don't always need your solution. If you can be present and listen, they will be able see that you love them and appreciate how much you care.

Even if they can't express their feelings in words; your silent presence will soothe them.

Even if you disagree with them, Validate Their Emotions

Your loved ones may be thinking or acting out of control. It can be difficult for loved ones to come around when they are provoked or go through a crisis.

You don't have agree with them in order to support their sentiments.

Human emotions can be either right or wrong. In some ways, emotions are rational because they are accompanied in part by reasoning and stories. If someone does not have the experience of being loved and has lived their entire life without it, it is easy to understand why they would react this way.

Your decision doesn't affect their emotional reality. They are, in you opinion, reacting excessively. What they don't grasp makes perfect sense.

Good news is that your disagreement with someone does NOT mean you are their enemy. You might validate their motives or opinions. Being a friend to someone with BPD doesn't necessarily mean you have to agree with them. However, you might still be able express your support for them and your opinions.

You may use phrases like, "I get that it's _____", or "I see from what your saying that right now you feel _____." You aren't lying or twisting ideas in this way. You only sympathize with their situation.

Take a look at your inner child

BPD sufferers have often suffered traumatizing and complicated childhoods. An inner wounded child still lives in them, longing to hear, be loved, and feel that they are appreciated. Sometimes we lose sight. We are able to see someone who is highly-functioning, creative, capable in other aspects of their lives. However, this doesn't mean that they have an unhealed wound. To love someone with BPD you need to be able recognize and treasure their inner child.

It's possible for them to suddenly fall into a childlike state after a heated debate. These moments will show you that they are the most injured or lost and not the healthiest. This becomes apparent when you consider their bad words and violent behavior. You also need to examine their body language. The yelling. shrinking. and shivering. They may say things that they regret later. Children may also yell if they aren't allowed to have their way.

It is difficult to maintain calm when you are under attack. As a parent, it may help to pretend that you are dealing primarily with a child. They are like a young child and have not yet learned to communicate their needs and desires. Therefore, their screams and shouts can be an indication that they need help.

Think about the emotional demands beyond your surface behaviors. You may be surprised at the deepest longings you feel that result from previous deprivation.

Be mindful that the actions of your loved one are designed to keep them from extreme emotional anguish. They are not meant to injure and manipulate them. Befriending someone with BPD can help you see beyond the circumstances and to recognize the grief, love, and pain behind them.

BPD-related love and support.

Not being a victim or a victim of abuse is enough to show compassion and empathy. Not all people with BPD must be loved.

There is a happy compromise where you can be kind and set healthy boundaries, while still being compassionate. A young person may need you to be strong and kind while still being compassionate.

It is often impossible to talk to someone in the heat, but logic and reason can still be useful. You can simply reiterate your bottom line calmly and firmly.

It is best to not walk away from them. You could be fueling their abandonment anxiety by allowing them to go it alone. It may be possible to start by clearly communicating the repercussions in non-punitive ways, such as "I know you feel _____, and want to be there for you." If you keep shouting or throwing objects, I will have five minutes to leave the room. Make no hollow threats. Keep saying what you said. You should also avoid trying to penalize or counter-attack.

If they feel calmer, then sit down together to form a plan.

A good crisis plan' is one that identifies their worst triggers, helps them through those times and avoids them from repeating themselves. It is not about them. You might also use this opportunity to bargain and express your needs. It's important to plan ahead so both of your demands can be met.

Respect yourself, while loving someone with BPD

BPD can be a love that is difficult to accept. It is possible to love someone with BPD and feel sorry for them but it is impossible to save them.

You might feel guilty or resentful. But continuing to have an unhealthy relationship will not fix it.

They are their friend, but you are your own person. BPD-related codependency shouldn't be a result of loving someone. You cannot change someone's past traumas, and you can't save them. For your inability to save, please don't feel sorry for yourself. You can be their greatest ally or supporter, but it is not your responsibility to their healing and progress.

If you are angry at being in this relationship, remember that you have the choice to stay or go. If you choose not to leave, do not punish them.

However, some people believe BPD cannot be cured. Numerous studies and stories show otherwise.

BPD is a condition that makes it difficult for people to relate to them. Many are extremely sensitive, intelligent, compassionate, strong and compassionate. BPD is a complex condition that requires the love of someone you care about to have the ability and talent to be there for them. But it also has its benefits and rewards. Your love and devotion will help them heal. It will be worth it in the end.

Chapter 5: The Importance Structure

And Routine In Your Daily Life

Your daily routines can be the secret to your destiny. Mike Murdock

Did you notice that your mother, dad, and caregivers had a schedule for you that looked like boundaries? You had meals at specific times throughout the day. There was a time that you could use television or computer, and there was a curfew. Many people would agree that teenagers, and children, need a structure and routine to develop healthy life skills. Routine is also crucial for creating and maintaining healthy habits that can be carried into adulthood. Parents, children, teens, and young adults all benefit from having a structure and routine to maintain a healthy balance throughout their day.

This book is designed to give you tools to manage your bipolar disorder. It also serves as a safe haven for you to visit when you feel that you do not deserve to be alone in this mad world. Remember, you are a part of this world. But the world isn't part of you. As I have repeatedly said, you are your own person. You are free to have bad days and good days, without having the world judge you. You might have found some of what I say frustrating. Friends and loved ones may have created a routine for your to follow. However, if freedom is your goal, you must learn how to create a strategy plan that fits with what you want. You are the one with the mental disorder and therefore have the right to be included in the planning.

Healthy Habits to Include in Your Daily Life

Habits are a part of every day that you live since birth. There were a few habits that you learned while you were pregnant. These included using your mother's bladder and kidneys as a pillow. Kicking her kidneys would let her know you were frustrated. And sucking your thumbs or fingers out when you finished with karate and ballet. These were habits that you had for about nine weeks. Some of these may have been continued after your birth. Your ability to cry when you're sad, hungry, or just wanting attention created new habits. There were many habits that you picked up throughout your childhood. Some you kept with you through adulthood, while others you dropped. Habits can be automatic and you don't often think about why and what you're doing. Sometimes you're conscious of creating good habits and other bad ones.

Before you create a routine it is necessary to first look at the items required to be part of the structure. These items also include our habits. I was able to find an article that a team of psychologists wrote about the importance habitual in people's behavior. It seems reasonable to conclude that our behavior affects our lives and the relationships that we have with our loved ones. The article states that each person's behavior is determined by their habits. Habits are often based on how we live our lives and how we interact. Merriam Webster's online dictionary gives many different definitions of what habits are. According to Merriam-Webster's online dictionary, habits are behaviors that are developed by repeated acts that result in a pattern of behavior (Merriam Webster).

How to Make and Keep Habits

Have you ever taken some time to think about your habits? You can make a list of all your habits--good, poor, and everything in-between--and reflect on their origins. Ask as many questions about why you have these bad habits as you like to uncover the truth. Then, decide if the habits are adding value to your life or hindering you from moving ahead. You may discover that you have a few habits you are using as a default setting. You can get rid of the unhealthy habits and add new ones that will benefit your mental well-being. This could trigger you because you are changing some part of what you know. But remember all the techniques from the previous chapters. Breathe and take it slow. And think about what the next chapter might bring.

Now that you're prepared for any scenario, it is time to teach you how to make good habits. I am as honest as ever with you about this: the art of creating new habits is not something you can do overnight. It is a long process that requires patience, persistence, and determination. Use the list that I made; concentrate on the things you want to change. And believe that you can and WILL prevail. I believe you. If someone can believe that your reign will be supreme, then so can you. Let's get you started in your quest to develop and maintain new and familiar habits.

The Habit Portal Preparation

This is the list that I had to create. I wanted to show you how to make the changes you want. I encourage you to add any new habits or tips to your list. Learning how to modify old habits will help you transition to new habits. Don't let go of an old routine to make space for a new, better one. Sudden changes can lead to anxiety, stress, and mixed emotions which could be a trigger for bipolar disorder. It is essential to take baby steps for your mental well-being and mental health. Always remember that babies and toddlers need to learn how crawl before they can walk. This is not the marathon. Your life is important.

* Only one habit is necessary to master.

* Assemble new habits onto existing ones.

* Be consistent with your daily lifestyle habits

* Set goals for yourself.

* Make reminders to help you keep practicing your habits.

* Turn your bad habits into a reward scheme.

You'll know when you've successfully adapted or modified your habits by the way you act without thinking. Your mind will adapt to the new additions. Your new habits will allow you to develop a rhythmic system that will prevent triggers from overwhelming your mind. Next is to make a routine. Remember that habits can help keep you grounded and give you the ability to dig in when it gets difficult.

Structure and Routine help keep triggers at bay

It may seem strange that I would choose habits to over routine or structure. But the truth is, habits need their own space. I wanted you to understand why healthy habits are important. And what they mean for your mental and physical health. It is possible that you have negative habits that I didn't address. I hope that you will begin to see how positive habits are beneficial for your life.

What is routine and structure? I've spoken of it and your therapist may have also mentioned it. A layman's definition can help you understand what you are being referred too. I understand and can help you to piece together the puzzle pieces. The Merriam Webster online dictionary says that a routine refers to a strategy or plan that has been created to guide people through a specific period (Merriam Webster. n.d.c). According to Merriam Webster's trusted dictionary, a structure means something that is consistent and that makes sense to all the participants (Merriam Webster.

Individuals with bipolar disorder must have a structured routine and structure in order to succeed. Routines can be further strengthened with the addition of habits that will help people achieve the goals they desire for self-satisfaction. Do you keep a journal and a pen? Let's get started by learning how to plan, make a routine, and implement those habits to help with managing any symptoms.

The Importance Of Building and Developing Bombproof Routines and Structures

Did you know that each day only contains 24 hours? You might be as surprised as I was when you found this piece of information. It is a fast-paced, highly competitive world. We must complete everything within a specific time. I don't like the blame game. Each person is responsible to set boundaries for their personal and professional lives. The world is made up of seven continents. Due to the global connectivity, it has become possible for individuals to work remotely in other countries. The 24-hour cycle of work becomes endless if one half of the globe is asleep while the other is awake and productive. We spend so much time trying to do as much as we can that we forget to take care of what is most important--ourselves!

I've witnessed my patients feel the pain on their faces when they realize they can not do everything that they wanted to when they woke in the morning. They are overwhelmed by the idea that they will have to make difficult or disappointing choices. This allows us to open the door we had closed and locked, that holds thoughts and preconceived notions. The chain reaction creates stress, worry, anger, and can trigger any number of triggers which could lead to a nuclear reaction. You don't require that nuclear reaction and neither do your neighbors. Because of this, structure and routine are important. Individuals suffering from bipolar disorder must have a daily to-do list. This lists the things they need to do and when. You may not think this is necessary if you don't fully understand what it is to be diagnosed with a mental disorder. But, to you--dear bipolar disorder patient--this will put a smile upon your face.

Make Your Own Routine
This is a time to establish or change a routine. Make sure you set aside time each day to plan ahead for next week. You will need to create a weekly plan.
To-Do List
* Make a list with everything you need, from the moment you wake-up until the time that you go to sleep.

* You may be surprised to find out how many of your habits are included on the list.

* Look at your habits to identify what needs to be altered and what would benefit from a cue.

* Take a look at your to-dos again to ensure you have everything, including recreation, chores, appointments, and activities.

Structure

Take a piece paper and make three columns. Then, write the headings for morning, noon, or evening. Make a list of items that you want to accomplish and arrange them in the right columns. I want to remind you that your routine will work for you, and not someone else's. The purpose of this structure is to help find and maintain stability and direction. This is an entirely new skill for you. When you become proficient at it, it will become second-nature.

Intentions

You now have columns that you have dressed with the items from your to-do checklist. You should now take note of your intentions when creating your routine. Let's take for example that "the Kitchen" is on the to-do listing. Now, you must describe what you want or require in the kitchen. It is possible to write under the heading "the kitchen" that you have to wash the dishes and run the dishwasher. You may also wish to wash the countertops and sweep up the floors.

Many routines are also time-based. People with mental illnesses may not be able to be given time frames. This is a potential stress trigger as it can encourage people who are obsessed with completing everything in a specified time. The risk of panicking, anxiety, or worrying that they won't do the right thing in the time they have been given could increase if they push beyond their set time limits. While I am

73

sensitive to those who require structure, I also realize that everyone requires some freedom and flexibility to let their minds wander.

Check out Your New Routine

To see how you feel, try your new routine for a couple of days. Then, take the time and make the changes you need. Don't worry about doing things differently to your usual routine. The unpredictable nature of life means that you cannot control how it turns out. Maybe a friend text you inviting you to coffee at the local café.

Your greatest gift to yourself is your trust in yourself. Be confident in yourself, and you will accomplish anything. I will give you many tools to make you feel lighter. I'm sure you'll feel more at home when you start seeing the possibilities in front. Everything will work together, and you'll feel worthy of being a member of this chaotic, fast-paced environment.

Your bipolar disorder can leave you feeling isolated and unloved. I know you're aware that the book has started to spark a new passion for you and your life. Let your flame shine brightly in your world, dear reader. You don't need to be ashamed, embarrassed or embarrassed to show the imperfections of others.

Addressing the Fear that You Will Be Abandoned And Rejected

A generous heart is always open to receiving our goings and comings. You don't have to worry about being abandoned when you are surrounded by such love. This is one of the most precious gifts true love gives--the feeling of belonging. -Bell Hooks

What is fear, exactly? Here is where I hit "Pause" and give you a formal definition from the trusted Merriam Webster online dictionary. Fear is an emotion which prepares your mind and body for potential negative energy reactions. It makes you more alert or prepares you for possible danger.

People are made to doubt their own worth by using emotions. A conversation between a bank clerk and a customer was something that made me smile. The cashier was smiling as she greeted her customer. Her bright whites sparkled as her smile glowed, and her green eyes were a highlight. She may have been having a bad day because she didn't smile back. Instead, the customer looked at the cashier with curiosity. She continued working and tried to engage in light conversation. The customer asked the cashier if she was always happy. The cashier answered: "I choose be happy because negativity doesn't exist." The world needs happier people, less anger, sadness and heartache. I don't think anyone should expect me to be happy. However, I know that I have plenty of happiness for everyone. That's what I needed to hear today. Thank you.

The world needs more understanding, and more happy people. It is impossible to know what someone is going though. These people could be labeled the same way as other people. I know that people do not want to face the facts and see health issues as a burden they prefer to ignore. People are afraid of contagious diseases that may result from compromised health. Are you familiar with the possibility of someone getting a neurobiological brain disorder, incurable illnesses, or mental health conditions by sharing a cup, kissing or using the same toilet? No.

It is possible to neutralize the fear of being abandoned or rejected

* Do your beliefs about the world being a better place beg for all emotions to be banned?

* Do You believe you would find it beneficial to have your emotions stored

in a safe before being thrown into Bermuda Triangle.

It would be so simple. It would take quite a while to get rid of all the different emotions. Our central processing units have many nerves. Each one serves a purpose and plays a part in our existence. This is how you have been exposed to short circuits and the side-effects that they can bring. While your brain may still be working and sending messages across the various parts of your bodies, you are now a survivor. You have been diagnosed bipolar disorder. You are aware that it isn't a death sentence. You know you can live to your hundredths if you keep yourself fit, healthy and active. As I said, you don't have to let bipolar disorder define your personality. Despite some difficulties, you are still the imperfect person you always were.

Do you recall how you arrived at your diagnosis? You, your family, or your friends were in great distress at that time. You didn't know what was really going on in your brain or why you were having difficulty communicating your true emotions. It is possible that you have caused hurt feelings in people you love and made statements you didn't intend to say. You may have tried everything to make things right in those early days. But fear had invaded your emotional boundaries. Fear set up shop, and has been living within the confines of your emotional boundaries--rent-free--ever since. It is time for fear to be expelled, or at most, neutralized. You must show fear who is truly in control of your mind palace.

The Reality of Abandonment or Rejection

I believe there are two types people living in the world. Some are known as loners. They don't like being crowded into their personal space. Which of these groups are you part?

It is safe for us to say that almost all human beings are pack animals. These are the people that need and want the love, support, and kinship of the people around them. They want to feel accepted and valued as "passe" members. These individuals could also feel the most afraid that the group will dissolve and they will be left behind. This could be seen as insecurity. Others might believe it is paranoia. These individuals are trying to repair a chemical imbalance and rewire their nerves. Even if they don't have any mental issues, they may not be able understand the whole process. They might not understand how to handle bipolar disorder and may create emotional triggers that can be harmful.

Individuals with bipolar disorder could find themselves in a difficult position when their close friends and family become distant. Your family and friends could recall all of your negative words and actions, including the mood swings and behaviors. Although you may not be aware of your bipolar disorder, it is possible for people with it to distrust you. They might try to shield themselves from you which creates a loop effect that keeps coming back for them. Fear, which is hiding within your emotional boundaries is enjoying your pain and insecurity. As your triggers start activating the alarms, your defenses become weaker and more vulnerable. Your emotional boundaries have been compromised by fear and negativity that have caused you to believe that your abilities are not worth being part of any group. Are you aware of the way your emotions play with your mind and body? These are the negative feelings that you can have because of your thoughts.

The truth is the fear that you will be abandoned or rejected is real. It doesn't matter if your family is part of a pack, or you are an isolated person; fear has real consequences. It can become even more severe when you feel abandoned or rejected by the people you care about. Fear-mongering thoughts often come from a place in which you may feel that you have been lost or replaced. Social media can fuel thoughts and emotions. You will scroll through your friend's page to see photos of friends' weekend trips that don't involve you. You can recall speaking with your friend on Friday and not hearing anything about going to the weekend. Images and thoughts start to swirl around your mind and you are trying desperately to make sense. You want your voice to be heard (thank goodness for mood stabilizers), yet you know it will come out of you mouth unfiltered. It's hard to feel loved when you are behind a dark wall. You phone your friend, and you wait for their thoughts on the weekend. But, they don't say anything. The brain's sensors start flashing but you still don't say much. While they are hurting you, understanding and realisation enter your mind palace.

Signs of Abandonment

We're quick to allow our emotions to control us and to let them run a few laps on the racecourse. Where did these thoughts come? This is not a thought that you have decided to wake up and fear that your mother, father, siblings or friends will abandon you.

One article suggests your fear of abandonment may be due to childhood experiences. A second article says that it can be caused by trauma later on in life. Memories are capable to rise from the dust or thick layers of dust in the archives. They can also be used to help you feel safe within your emotional boundary. The next task is to identify triggers that could cause you to lose the progress made towards your current point.

Are you curious if you might have abandonment problems? Many people around you and society may tell that you are desperate and are the poster child to abandonment. Let's look at the signs you might use to tell if your abandonment issues are present.

* Fear of a dear one abandoning or passing away

* Clinging to one-sided relationships because I need them

* falling for people who do not want to be committed.

* Feeling alone in my thoughts forever

* Feeling that there is no support

* Feeling my life is a living, breathing machine where people come and leave as they please

* I am afraid that I will rely more on people than I should

* Feeling as though people are in this life for the benefits they can offer me. However, once the well is dry, they become dry and leave me with the mess.

Reclaiming Your Beliefs

It is now that you can turn your fears about being left alone and high-and-dry into positives. You may also want to hear another one of mine. This little secret can only be revealed if you have a mirror or a front-facing camera. Do you see the mirror or your smartphone? Do you see the person in front of you? Wave at that person and openly welcome them into your home. If they look back at them, it is because they are afraid. Let them know that they don't have to be afraid being alone. Tell them they are incredible in every way. Tell them that you will always be there for them, and they will never feel lonely. Use your phone or mirror to talk to yourself whenever you feel fearful and alone. People might think you've lost some marbles. I don't know about them, but I would rather talk with my reflection, than run around with rage and anger and fury. Because your boundaries have been breached, I can assure you that you won't risk mood episodes.

Reframing How You Think

Negativity is something we all face. Children are fond of saying "I can't make it" when asked to do something. Adults use this phrase when confronted with challenging situations at work or at home. Positive affirmations and positive words are essential to overcome negativity. You might consider adding this to the list. Consider a habit you already have, add a cue and claim your reward. It might be difficult, but there is no harm in trying something new. It keeps your mind busy, stops you from worrying about situations that take your energy and can set off your triggers. That is something you want.

I want to share a technique that will help your go through negative thoughts with a fine-toothed comb. Make a note of all negative thoughts, examine their roots, and set yourself a challenge. This exercise will enable you and all those in your circle to better understand yourself and help you. This exercise is for everyone, as they'll also be able to spot possible trigger warnings. You should be open about your self-assessment. This is for your own benefit and will eventually help you become independent and self-sufficient.

Take Notice of Patterns

You cannot see negative thoughts. You can however identify negative beliefs. These are connected to your feelings and emotions.

* A sense of helplessness
* Feeling unlovable

* Feelings that are not worthy or worthy of happiness
* Because of past actions, you have been a bad character.
* You don't deserve to be loved, respected, or appreciated.
* You're a disappointment to all around you

Analyzing the Origin of Negative Thoughts

This is your chance, to uncover the source of your negative thoughts. Ask yourself some questions to discover where your negative thoughts are coming.

* Do they have roots in your childhood
* Were your cousins bullying you as a youngster?
* Did your grandfather tease or teasing you?
* Were the only children you had before having a sibling?
* Did an ex-employer treat you with disrespectful language?

* Did you witness something that scared or intimidated you?

Although everyone will answer different self-assessment question, I can give you examples that can be modified to your particular narrative and circumstances.

Take on a challenge

The negative beliefs and questions that have been asked have been addressed. Now it is time for you and your family to address the negativity that threatens overwhelm you with episodes of depression or hypomania. This is the time to stand tall, get out of your way, and affirm that no negativity can stop you from moving forward. I'll be watching from the sidelines, encouraging you and weeping with pride. This is how much faith in your ability for managing your bipolar disorder.

You must practice. Remember, you will need patience, practice and time. You will learn how to think before your react. It is obvious that thoughts will always come into your mind. But you can take control of them by hitting the pause button. Then, think about what negative thoughts might be. Let's consider a possible scenario, and then accept the challenge.

"I feel as though I don't have anyone to support me."

* Why would someone feel like that?

* Have you ever heard anyone say they wouldn't stand by you?

* What evidence is there to show that you don't have the support you need?

"What should we do?"

Examine your thinking and take a step out of the situation. Find three positive aspects in your surroundings to overcome your negative feelings.

* I can see my spouse or family member admiring me.

* I see that some chores that I didn't complete today have been completed.

* I see the arms of supportive and caring people waiting for you to reach out and grab them.

Removing the Oxygen Thief from your Emotional Boundary

Fear is an oxygen thief. It holds you down until you can't move or feel any movement. Panic sets in. It overtakes you and fills up your mind in negativity. You do everything you can to counter those negative thoughts. However, fear has a way to ruin all that hard work. Your bipolar disorder becomes worse, your sensors become vulnerable, and it is back to square one when you learn how to identify your thoughts. Doubt mixes with fear, and you will believe you are the subject of the next conversation. It is as if everyone in the room is looking at you.

STOP! STOP! You will not entertain fear, doubt, anxiety, or any other negative-inducing emotion in order to upset a very stable applecart. Practice some of your calm exercises, such as yoga, meditation, or breathing. If thoughts get to you, distract yourself. Go for a walk or dance in the garden. Or, write in your journal. Remind yourself that you are in complete control at all times. I bet you didn't know fear doesn't have arms, legs or a voice. Fear is an invisble force that can't be physically hurt, so it is okay to resist it, and you can banish it with whatever means you like.

Chapter 6: How To Get To Know Me

I believe everyone is unique. Each person is unique and that is what makes us beautiful. It would be boring for us to all be the same. -Tila Tequila

As I said, having a diagnosis for positive bipolar disorder doesn't define you. Yes, people are willing to talk. Yes, people will point fingers. People will make assumptions. Can you stop people becoming obsessed with you? Unfortunately, you can't. However, the good news is that this isn't about anyone else or their opinions. This is about you, your "struggle", and your journey. You are the one who struggles to find your place in the world. Each chapter has affirmations. You are exactly what you were made to be. You are your best friend. Who better knows you than you? No one.

I have observed that people fight for the spotlight. They want to stand out, be seen as knowledgeable and helpful, even if it contradicts what has been done. Everyone seeks the acknowledgment, the praise, or the verbal compliments for their achievements and helpfulness. Some may claim that they are trying to be too prominent at work, school or in their friend group. Others might also agree and add that their insecurity is a problem and they need to be acknowledged for it.

Individuals suffering from bipolar disorder do not go out seeking attention. They live with a large microscopic camera that watches every movement for signs of manic episodes or mood swings. Individuals with bipolar disorder have a special place on my heart. Due to my personal connection with bipolar disorders, I'm not biased. My family and my patients make me proud to see the great progress they have made. I am a proud advocate of individuals with neurobiological and other mental disorders. Individuals diagnosed with bipolar disorder (or are currently in the process) need encouragement and support. Everyone is welcome in this world, regardless of their gender, age, mental health or financial situation. Everyone has the ability to walk, breathe, and be who and how they choose.

Steps to Finding Me

You should be proud to be who you are. Remember that you are unique because of all your imperfections. Want to see how unique you truly are? Examine your hands, palm-side up. Take a closer look at what you are doing. Do you see the lines? Are there circles? It is your distinctive branding. This is what differentiates you and the other seven billion human beings on this planet. There are no fingerprints that are identical to yours. This is a reminder both to you and to everyone else that each person has their own identity. The opening of the chapter contains a powerful quote: "If everyone is the same, it would just be boring."

I encourage my patients, friends, and family to find their identity. I'm amazed by the beauty and creativity of Instagram. Instagram influencers provide links and discount codes for the clothes they wear, their hair products and their food. A couple of days later, when you go through their profiles, you see pictures of people in the same clothes. It's hard for me to see how it is worth being someone other than you are.

This is Who You Want to Be

People diagnosed with bipolar disorder may feel excluded from the support and guidance they need. Diagnoses bring a huge amount of baggage. People feel confused, condemned, and overwhelmed by self-doubt. The brain is in danger of a new short circuit because people aren't sure what to do next. Your life as it was has been changed by bipolar disorder. You may believe that your life is over. To live out your remaining days, you'll probably need a padded bedroom. You may even feel that all you value--your identity, dignity, and the person who you were before the diagnosis - is going to disappear.

Refer to Chapter 3, which discusses the topic of containing negative thoughts and feelings. Remember that your bipolar disorder does NOT define you. Look at your diagnosis as a chance to redefine yourself, not to conform to others' expectations. Don't try to be someone you don't know, such as a celebrity or a social media influencer. Why would you want a role model for someone already in existence? Let me ask this question. I'll share a list with benefits that will show you why it is important to be you.

* Fortified relationships within your circle

* A strong sense to follow your passions throughout life

* The belief that everything you set your mind to do is unique and authentic to you, and your passion

Understanding your life is not about having fancy gadgets and bows. It's about simplicity and knowing who you are.

* Accepting that you do not need a bipolar diagnosis to hinder your personal growth

My question was simple: "I don't think I want to be another person, because I only know what they are experiencing." I do not know what they are feeling. I choose authenticity, redesigning myself and being the best me I can be.

* No means no.

* Get rid if you feel that it doesn't bring value to your daily life.
* Don't sacrifice values for the sake or others.
* Always be truthful
* Stand up for what is right.
This is who I should really be
First, get rid off any negative thoughts. Although this may sound difficult, it is possible. One of my patients mentioned to me that her mother taught them to destroy negative thoughts with kindness. Those thoughts do not reflect on your character, who or what you should be. You can only be the person you have been meant to become if you have walked through a forest of thorns to find a field covered in moss. No one-- no thought or individual--has the power to hinder your efforts to manage and cope successfully with your bipolar disorder.

Let's now look at how we can accumulate negative thoughts in our jars. We can then close the lid tight and kick it so that it falls into an active volcano. There it will bubble up, boil and finally disintegrate. It may seem impossible, but you can dream big, even if your mental state is not. What can we do in a non-fantasy universe to yield similar results.

* Get rid of negative thoughts.

* Change how you think. If you think that you are stupid for making a stupid error, correct yourself quickly to counter that negative.

* Accept your imperfections. Everyone is imperfect.

* Self-care is important. Don't let others tell you what to do.

* Triggerwatch: Rearrange your trigger radars so they can detect triggers, before they crash your emotional boundary.

This is me--Newer and Better

The pieces of this puzzle are finally starting to click together. Feeling at peace knowing you are worthy of being exactly who you are has brought you joy. It gave you hope that you can be the architect of your own thoughts. Each page is filled with affirmations. Your identity has been acknowledged and you can now manage your bipolar disorder. You already know that the weight of being diagnosed with bipolar disorders will always be on your back. You are no longer carrying the weight of bipolar disorder. Your body will feel relief when it realizes that someone else is aware of the burden. This can help you to reduce anxiety.

I don't want anyone to feel lost now that they have rediscovered themselves. Keep a list listing your values. Be reminded regularly of your beliefs. Make a list of what you believe. Then, ask yourself questions about your beliefs. The following list is a glimpse at what your values or beliefs might look like.

*

* Caring
* Loving
* loyal
* Intuitive
* Proficient
* passionate
* open-minded
* Motivational
* understanding

Rely on the Self-Esteem

You now know who you are. You know that you are yourself. It is a habit that you repeat to make yourself believe what you are reading about yourself. You are the most important individual in your life. The confidence you have built for you is indestructible. You are aware that you are still a work-in-progress and that you don't have the right to rush. Every human being on earth has a purpose. Many people end up getting lost along the way to the spot marked X or your treasure. Others get so focused on finding X, they get lost. There are others who set out with a purpose. Take breaks, obstacles, and downtime into account and you will get to the spot X. They might look a little worn out, wary, and broken, but they succeeded and conquered what was set before them.

Let's take a closer look at a few ways to help you identify your X marks. These are the places that will guide you on your journey towards finding, keeping, and maintaining your true self. This exercise is also great to do in a group with family or friends who may need some guidance. The sky is your limit, the world's your oyster, and there are no limits to what you can accomplish. Ideas to inspire you include:

* It doesn't matter if you are afraid of silence. Simply close your eyes and meditate.

* Be who you really want and put all your positive beliefs in this space.
* You don't have the ability to do everything well; you are not competing against others.
* Ask questions. Be open to all feedback.

Making amends and rebuilding relationships that are damaged

Forgiveness doesn't mean giving up on the possibility that the past could change. It means accepting the past as it is, and making use of this moment to help you move on. -Oprah Winfrey

I am often struck by the thought that if there was an option to "rewind", we could go back in time and alter the outcome or prepare the present for the future. I would have made a plan to start Patricia's Gas Savings Fund if I had known in my youth about the gas price. I may be an eternal optimist that looks for the silver in every storm, but I'm also realistic.

My book, Overcoming Narcissistic Abuse: Your Freedom from Emotional Abuse (F.R.E.E. Guide to Empowering Youself, Breaking From Abuse and Achieving Peace. And finding Closure. While I would love to have the ability to change the future of my life, I know that I wouldn't be where today helping people navigate their lives with all these educational opportunities. This chapter has one message from my book:

You cannot make yesterday different. Yesterday has already passed and there's nothing you can do. You cannot do anything for tomorrow because you don't know what tomorrow will bring. The best place to live is today. The memories of yesterday can be used to create the foundation for tomorrow. Today, however, is a gift to you.

(Natpikia.2022, Chapter 5, Baby Steps., para. 3)

I would like to introduce you guilt. This is another of the squatters who have invaded your emotional boundaries. Guilt might not be able to speak for you, but it can remind you of the things that make your life difficult. Guilt likes to explore your subconscious to uncover hidden thoughts. Guilt may remind you about something you have done or said during a manic episode. Guilt is a time thefter who doesn't care what happened. However, it will bring out retirement, remove the dust and push it around your brain to remind. It's time for guilt to prove who the true master in your mind palace. You're going to place guilt in a jar to silence it.

The Past is the Place It Belongs

The heading states it all: the past is exactly where it belongs--in fact, it's in the present. You might have experienced mood episodes before being diagnosed with bipolar disorder. You might have hurt someone you cared about. Because you didn't know what to say or do, people may have been alienated by your initial actions. It was never your intention harm others, alienate or push them away. The brain short circuit destroyed a vital part of your mouthpiece. This filter controls your ability to think and speak before your brain does. This is where guilt begins to gather every piece of information--ammunition--it can find to torment you when you begin mending broken bridges.

You cannot return to the past. Nobody knows how to time travel. To move forward, it is the best thing for everyone. While you can't reverse or change hurtful words or unforgiven actions, it is possible to make amends, seek forgiveness, or rebuild relationships that are damaged. This action will almost certainly increase guilt because it will lose power over your emotions. How do you reconcile with something you may have said or done in the past, even if it was not your intention? I am glad that you asked. I would love the opportunity to help you make peace with past mistakes and move forward in your life.

Accepting that You Can't Change The Past

It's time for forgiveness. It is time to make amends with those you may have hurt, pushed away, or intentionally hurt. Some people may have excommunicated and no longer want to be friends with you. Others might be hesitant to trust your motives. You shouldn't feel guilty for someone's feelings. While you can't control their emotions, you have a deep desire to make amends. Some may argue that you are selfish, and they want to clear your mind. Others might say the damage is done and not be interested in hearing any explanations. Others may be just as happy to give you another chance at making amends and offer to help you. It is impossible keep everyone happy.

You will want to keep the "others," because they believe and trust you. They are the ones who can see the impact of your actions. They are also the ones that will gladly help you build bridges. They have been waiting for your return in the shadows.

Feedback

Ask your family and close friends to share what has hurt them. Ask them to give you feedback to help you continue your lifelong journey. You should accept their feedback and guidance without taking offense.

Accept What You Can't Do

This may seem difficult to grasp for most people, however it is vital. Keep in mind that rocks and sticks may cause broken bones. They can also leave scars, bruises, and other permanent injuries that will eventually fade. The superglue will stick to the words for an eternity. Accept responsibility, accept your apology, and promise to be mindful of the future.

Get Rid Of Your Redundant Baggage

This is the perfect opportunity to separate the "some", "others" as previously stated. People who are unwilling to forgive or extend an olive branch for you don't deserve a spot in your life. Your true circle includes people who will not only stand beside you but also be critical of you.

Ho'oponopono

I was introduced by someone who was having difficulty forgiving people for hurting their feelings. The Ho'oponopono is thought to have originated in Hawaii. This mantra is designed to help you forgive people and allow them to forgive. The mantra is composed of four phrases. This mantra can be used as many times per day as you'd like and in any situation. The mantra asks that you repeat each phrase in any order. Consider the situation or person that you are speaking about for a while between each phrase. You might consider including this mantra in your day to help you manage your emotions, thoughts and feelings. It will also help during times when alarm bells sound and triggers begin to set in.

Please forgive.

I am sorry.

I love you.

Thank you.

Restructuring   Storm-Damaged Destruction In the Aftermath Of Bipolar Disorder

This chapter and possibly the entire book is important in helping you deal with and manage your bipolar disorder. This milestone was an important one in this journey. Next, we will create a mosaic out of the bits and pieces left from our new venture. To help you get your new groove with bipolar disorder, you have a team of family members and friends. These people have been hand-selected and can be your glue to help you stay on track.

You may feel guilty even though you were forgiven by your friends and family. You might feel that your friends and family don't trust or respect you. Perhaps you are having difficulty communicating with people because guilt is sitting beside fear and filling up your mind full of cotton balls. These are natural responses especially after you have experienced trauma like a diagnosis with bipolar disorder. This is nothing you should be ashamed of as it's something that you can't control. It was impossible to know the truth about your mind. You didn't understand that you were accidentally hurting people who want to help.

Rebuilding Trust

Trust is the core of relationships in families, friendships and business. One party or several can compromise a relationship's foundation. If trust is broken through hurtful words or acts, betraying another person by spreading false rumors or telling lies, cheating on your partner, or theft, then a relationship may be in a compromised state. The good news? Trust can be rebuilt. Although it might take some time, you can still show those you've hurt that you care about your relationship and offer them help. It's worth the effort to show family and friends you will fix what has gone wrong. Let's have a look at some options that you could use to build a mosaic of broken pieces.

Apologize

We use sorry a lot. "Sorry," I found, is a common scapegoat word. People will use it to repeat the same offenses again, even though they don't realize that sorry comes with sincerity. Without sincerity, there is no way to be believed. The good news about this is that those who know you well will recognize when you are trying too hard to be convincing. An open and sincere apology comes from the heart. The letter you write to those who have hurt you and their families is another way to express your regret. This type of apology is useful when you don't wish to have personal interactions with someone. Share your heart and tell them that you love them.

Collaborate

It is possible to work with your family members and friends to fix your relationship. It is important to have someone to support you. This will enable people who have hurt you to see the positive changes you are making and also help them to see the hard work and commitment you put into your relationship.

The Foundation of the Future

The future is unpredictable and planning for it can be difficult. Learning anything from the global pandemic which broke out unexpectedly, spread like wildfire and left a trail of destruction that left the world reeling, you will know that tomorrow is not certain. As the eternal optimist I am, I've had to retrain myself to see the near-term instead of the far future. You cannot change the history, but you can forgive for what has happened. You can learn from the past and make a new start today. This is a consistent practice that everyone should do to keep their slate clean.

Show your love and support for the people in you life that you are working hard at gaining their trust. Allow them to see your progress, and they will be a part of it. Show them how to build their own future and allow them to be part of the multi-laned highway.

Open Line of Communication

Trust is an inextricable two-way street. You must give what is due. You might say you want to trust your family and friends, but you must also trust them. Your circle and friends don't know your feelings. All they know about you is what they've seen in your actions. It is time for you to invite your warriors into your fold and establish trust. Make sure you have your resources, as well as a copy. You must speak with honesty, truth, and your heart. You are free to share as much as or as little information as you need about your circumstances. This is your journey. Your guardian angels are there to help you, if you're willing to.

Support System

It is possible to share your bipolar disorder diagnosis among the people in your circle of friends and family. This will help you build a support system. When you are experiencing mood swings that cause you to feel unable to do tasks, a support group is there to help. My patients told me that their support groups are like a village full of chickens who help when they need it most. You don't know when mood episodes can strike suddenly and overwhelm your life. Your support system knows how to talk to you. Offer to cook dinner, do your grocery shopping, or pick up your kids from school. It's okay for your village to support you.

Ask for help

Never be afraid or embarrassed to ask for help. For those who have made the commitment to being there in difficult times, it is essential that they maintain an open channel of communication. Even though it might be difficult to ask for assistance, it is not impossible. You might be too sensitive and expect

negativity and rejection, even though you are still making amends. There may be a reason why you don't ask for help.
* The fear of being rejected
*Regrettable
* Not to be an inconvenience
* Shame
* embarrassment
It's okay to accept that people won't be able or willing to help. They may still be able the next day. I spoke to someone that said that they don't have transportation to shop for necessities. They explained that people always tell them to shop online and have it shipped to them. They explained that their friends are often unable to find what they need and they start experiencing cold sweats. The majority of the time, the friend can make the quick-stop stop. However, there are times when they might need to call the friend and ask if they could do it tomorrow. One person I spoke to stated

that while the friend had never refused to help them, it does not stop the fear and panic of the no answer. My advice would be to always ask, and be ready to accept both positive and adverse responses.

Bipolar Disorder: The Expectations

This section of the chapter will guide you in how to talk to your loved ones and to make them realize that you are still just the same person. The only difference is that their brain functions differently and that you need to be loved and understood. It is possible to leave this section unopened and spread it around your house, in the bathroom, kitchen, or bedroom. Guests may get a glimpse of what the author wants to say, but may not be able to hear. The decision about how you want to share your information is completely up to the individual.

I have removed my kid gloves, but you may have them in your fanny pack, ready to comfort and offer advice or words of affirmation. They might not be able or willing to listen to your expectations. Did you realize that every parent has to cut the apron strings which allows their chickens to fly free? Bipolar disorder can lead to your loved ones wrapping you up in bubble wrap and protecting, while you just want to show everyone that you are capable of finding your feet. Let's discuss what expectations you can set for your family and close friends following a diagnosis of bipolar disorder.

Helping them

I mentioned having an open line to communicate with your family and close friends. But it is essential that this line remains open and clear from all debris. This new way is for you to communicate with them. They need to know how to respond to a mood episode. You want them as educated as possible and to be ready to assist you when you are experiencing symptoms. You should keep reminding your loved ones and friends that your bipolar disorder does NOT define who you are or what your character is. Instead, they should consider it an addition to their life.

Education

If this book has been helpful to you and your circumstances consider sharing it your family and close friends. Ask them questions about what is going on inside of you and why your senses seem to be heightened. A greater number of people will understand the daily struggles of bipolar disorder and be more open-minded, understanding, and compassionate. Add in the reminder that bipolar disorder can be contracted, and it is not an attention-seeking scheme to gain sympathy. This is a very serious condition that can be debilitating and many people are stuck with it.

Can Relationships Survive

It doesn't mean your relationship status must end or be labeled "it is complicated" due to a diagnosis of bipolar disorder. Every relationship will have its ups or downs. Some relationships are more difficult and require patience and understanding. A relationship with someone with bipolar disorder is possible. Both parties will have to work hard. Every "problem", has a solution. Let's have a look at some of the helpful options you might consider to help your relationships thrive.

* Counselling
* A family member, partner, or relative is involved in the treatment options
* self-care

What NOT TO SAY

I have already mentioned that many people do not have filters when they offer unrequested advice or talk about things they don't know. It is well-known that people are quick to say whatever they like to make themselves seem knowledgeable, even if they don't really understand the situation of another person. Most often, the person seeking the "advice," wants to pull their hair or slap their shin. This action can be stopped by the stigmatism and the ramifications of bipolar disorder. Breathe. Be calm. Breathe. Get out of your way.

Let's take a look a list of statements people don't want you to hear.

* Stop looking to make excuses!

* Are you coping okay?

* You don't necessarily need to get stressed.

* You have control over your happiness

* Is that normal? You have been like that for way too much.

* Do you know if your medication works? You are too strung.

* Make lifestyle changes such as exercising more and controlling how much you eat.

* You are not looking for attention.

This is a list of lovely affirmations that are bestowed to the heads and shoulders of bipolar disorder sufferers. Friends and family should be careful about what they say. They should also ensure that their filters are cleaned regularly.

Be aware of symptoms

While I have previously covered the symptoms and signs of bipolar disorder I will also include it here for a refresher.

Manic episodes may appear as:

* Elevated moods
* energetic
* Restless
* irritable
* aggressive
* talking rapidly
* Overactive imagination
* unable to sleep

Depressive episodes may present as:
* waves of sadness
* Anxiety
* lower energy levels
* Unable to sleep, oversleeping
* no appetite
* Self-harming tendencies
* Suicidal thoughts
* Disinterestedness in activities
The Severity Untreated Bipolar Disorder
This is another topic that I have discussed in previous chapters. However it is important not to forget the importance for being diagnosed by a physician. The symptoms described in the preceding section will intensify and become more severe over time. Many times, people who have never been diagnosed will feel overwhelmed, afraid, and frustrated. Imagine riding a roller coaster at Six Flags Disneyland. The ride takes you around in loops, experiencing drops, slowing and speeding up. This is what a person with

bipolar disorder might feel. These thoughts will cause them to drive people away, hurt and even convince themselves that the whole world is better without them.

Researchers at the National Institute of Mental Health have confirmed the theory that individuals with bipolar disorder can experience manic episodes that last up to seven consecutive days. Intervals vary from a few minutes to several hours per day to almost every day. Depressive episodes may last as long as two weeks. Both of these episodes can last up to two weeks. It is crucial that a professional diagnoses the patient. These episodes could cause psychosis. The individual may become delusional, and be subject to hallucinations.

Uplifting displays of Encouragement

I am going on a limb to say that the best positive display for someone with bipolar disorder would be to begin taking the medication as prescribed by their doctor. This is something I cannot stress enough and it is something your family and friends should all see, hear and understand. You are the most important person on your planet, and deserve the best that you can give. More people need to be understanding, compassionate, and open to all people.

I am sharing some words of affirmation that can help you feel good and be loved. It is worth your time to write or print affirming words and phrases. Decorate with words that will lift you up in times of need.

* You have a community around you.

* You are loved.

* Don't give up when the going gets difficult

* True friends will support you through bad days.

* I may not always understand what you are going though, but I will always be there for you.

* It is worthwhile.
* Don't let your disorder define yourself.
* You can be imperfect--a diamond in a rough.
Calming Tools
This section is an additional reminder of how your loved one can help you through a manic episode. The entire book is full with useful tools, tips and important information to aid anyone dealing with neurobiological and mental health conditions. This book could also be beneficial to self-help mental health wellbeing checkups.

Maintain your daily routine.
* Follow the sleep schedule.
* Limit or avoid the consumption of alcohol.
* Avoid illegal drugs
* Follow the doctor's orders and take the prescribed medication.
* Encourage daily exercise

* Set realistic goals.
* Attend therapy.
* Yoga is a good practice.
* Develop deep breathing techniques.
* Take pleasure in therapeutic massages.
* Meditation is a good practice.
* Keep the Ho'oponopono mantra in mind.

Be open to sharing your feelings with your loved ones. There is no reason to feel ashamed to tell your loved ones what you are feeling. They must understand what you are going though. They are there because you choose to have them by your side, and not because it is necessary. They have chosen to be there for your mental health and to assist you in managing and coping with your bipolar disorder. Suicidal thoughts and self harming conversations should always be considered seriously. These types of thoughts, discussions and feelings should not be minimized or ignored. It is impossible to know what you are going through at this moment. If you feel the need for help, please call your therapist.

Are you prepared for some good news concerning the future outlook on your diagnosis of bipolar disorder. Let's move to the next chapter. In this chapter you will learn that not all the talk about living a normal and happy life is just talk. As I mentioned, every problem has a solution. Every negative is accompanied by a positive.

Chapter 7: A Future That Fits You

You can search all the universe looking for someone who deserves your love and affection more than you do. That person will not be found anywhere. You are just as worthy of your affection and love as anyone else. -Buddha

Although I don't like to say "I said so", it is true. Buddha, a wise individual, knew that I would be writing a book in the future. He therefore decided to give me a quote. You are the most valuable person in your universe. It's easy to put yourself last to ensure everyone is happy. Without taking care of your own health, you will not be able serve, love, and provide care to others. I have granted you the freedom to be selfish. It's okay to use that two letter word that everyone uses, but you should not take offense when you do. This manipulative strategy of using two-letter words to fuel emotions and set off triggers which negatively affect your mood is called "the two-letter word". You cannot expect people to do the impossible. Say NO to people who take without offering you something in return. Say no when you feel the need for listening to your body, mind and soul.

A diagnosis of positive bipolar disorder does NOT mean that you should stop dreaming and pursuing your goals. Your brain wired differently than others, which means your brain faces challenges. I don't remember if anyone ever said it but challenges are good. They keep you sharp and on your toes. You are forced to reflect on your thoughts and actions, which can help you be more mindful of everything around. We have almost reached the end of our journey together, and are approaching the light at each end of that tunnel that I promised. Before I wrap this book with invisible bows, sprinkle it with glitter and forget about cleaning up, there is one other thing that I want to do. I want you see how using NO can create a new universe where your world revolves around you and your requirements.

Kindness is essential for yourself

I cannot even imagine what your experience has been since your bipolar diagnosis. Each patient had a different experience when they were first diagnosed with mental illness. One patient felt they were walking in dark, damp corridors. Another person described feeling confused and dazed. There were others who felt relief from the diagnosis, but were afraid to live in a society with no understanding of their condition. Others have said that the diagnosis robbed them of their dignity and self-worth.

I listen carefully to my patients. But, what I find most important is the pain they are experiencing. I get them with cracks, some even broken. With patience and understanding, they begin to patch the cracks by using filler. Broken ones then use bondingglue to put them back together. This chapter has special meaning to me as it contains filler and bonding adhesive, as well tools to help those who feel justified because of their mental illness. Get up, stretch out your chest and take a deep breath. Then, regain what you lost-- your dignity, your ability to live happy lives, and more.

Rebuilding Your Self-Esteem. Strengthening your Confidence

You might want to acknowledge that you can be your worst enemy. I am stating this in love, because you don't see or believe there is any goodness in you. You see your mistakes as failures or disappointments. And you fear that you will never achieve anything. You should not allow your bipolar disorder or depression to hold you back from reaching your emotional limits. Consider the positive affirmations I provided you with. Believe them. It is time to take back what your diagnosis of bipolar disorder stole from you: the inability to see your self as worthy. The key ingredient to self-esteem is confidence. Together, you can see the great in yourself.

Because you are worthy, tell yourself. You can make your self-esteem manifest and then send it out to the universe. It will be clear to everyone that your bipolar disorder is not going to take control of your life or turn it upside-down. Your bipolar disorder will be under your control if you take the initiative and stand up for yourself.

Show Kindness To Yourself

I don't know much about you, but it bothers me when people treat my like I am an object. Many people forget to use their filters and the words they produce are not flattering. Stop those people and remind them of your feelings. You can also tell them you will walk away if the disrespect continues. These are some questions you might want to ask me:

* Why would you treat yourself with disrespect and indifference?

* Where's your filter when you speak to yourself?

* Why do people think so little of themselves?

It is important to keep in mind that your bipolar disorders are an active part you. Be more mindful of yourself. This means that you must filter how you think, react, and act in order to avoid any potential problems. It takes just one thought, feeling or emotion to trigger alarm bells in your brain and set off mood episodes that overwhelm you. I have a simple exercise that you can add to your diary. It's something you can do at least 100 times a day. Every house has at least one mirror, which you may walk past many times. Take a deep, long look at your reflection the next time that you pass it. Smile at you. Remind yourself that you are an amazing person. Believe that you are beautiful or attractive. Tell yourself that you are a good-looking person.

Accepting Your Flaws

I have mentioned before that no two people look the same. I discussed how each person is unique. Everyone is special in their own way. Your bipolar disorder distinguishes you from someone with an immune condition or someone with a crooked smile. A person being called different does not automatically mean they are better, worse or less than you. Your "differentness", however, is a sign that you will have different experiences in life than those with no mental health concerns. But, just because you are "flawed" doesn't mean you shouldn't live your life. Accept all your flaws, warts or not, and strive to be the perfect imperfection of yourself.

Increase your Self-Esteem, Confidence and Self-Esteem

To get rid of all the negative thoughts and feelings you've accumulated prior to and/or after your diagnosis of bipolar disorder, it will take a lot more effort, patience, and dedication. It is hard work and something no one can help. Even though others may try, your thoughts, actions, or situations will remain ingrained in you. They will wait until the right moment to get out of your head and start playing. Let's discuss some self-esteem and confidence-boosting suggestions:

* Identify and highlight your strengths.
* Be patient and kind.
* Create positive relationships and be open to others who would like to be in your lives.

* Try a new activity once a week, or every other month. This will help you build your habits.

* Add that two-letter term to your vocabulary.

* Set goals, and achieve your tasks.

* Use your morals as a guide to doing what is right.

* Don't be afraid to take control of your life.

* Stand up for what is right.

* Do what it says you will do and not what you should.

* It's okay to let other people's opinions be your guide.

* Feel happy, smile more, share your joy, and be happy for those around you.

Letting go is a powerful way to heal

Would you rather continue your journey while avoiding the burden of the world and your bipolar diagnoses? This is an opportunity to free yourself from the burdens that prevent you moving forward. I have already mentioned it, so you must be able to see and believe in the importance of being an independent person. I can't stress enough that bipolar disorder isn't a death sentence. With the right treatment, therapy and life skills you can and will live a long and happy life. This book is a good example of all the possibilities you have for your life. It will allow you to be more free and able to explore new areas. I know your family members will want to wrap cotton wool around you. But, I also know you like the sound of others clucking. I am here to remind you that it is okay not to control. It's okay for loved ones to let you know they don't have any worries about you. Reassure them (and yourself) that you will reach out to them if necessary.

Your safety net is comforting. But every bird needs to leave its nest. It doesn't matter if you hold onto the past or are afraid to step out in faith. Fear should not stop you from living the current life. Let's talk about what you can to help you get rid off your attachments, and avoid the guilt.

Meditate

This practice has been repeatedly mentioned and it is truly amazing. It teaches people how to connect to themselves and discover a way to hear what their minds, bodies and souls have to say. There's nothing better that getting to know yourself and listening carefully to what your soul has to say, without the pressure of the outside world. Learn to step into a soundproof bubble, blocking out distractions that could otherwise remind you of who you are--hopeless.

Acceptance

It is important to remember that you can't control everything. Although you might claim that you have accepted your bipolar diagnosis, there is a part of you that hopes it will go away. Research and science both confirm that you will live with a bipolar disorder diagnosis for the rest. Accept what is impossible to change and take the best from the future.

Befriend the Person on the Mirror

Make friends with someone who looks at you in the mirror. That friend is the one you can trust to support you through tough times. This friend is your voice of reason and conscience. This is the friend that you want by your side throughout all of life. Tell your friend how much you appreciate them. And thank them for being part of your life.

The Past

This is another thing I've spoken about. It's okay that the past is forgotten. This is the moment you can put an end to yesterday's past and see that it has been overturned. Yesterday will give the tools to make your day successful. Archive yesterday to live for today.

Journaling

This is another one that I have used, recommended and loved. It's a therapeutic way to take your thoughts out of your head and it also serves to end negative feelings. This is another exercise that I often share with people: letter writing. If someone has hurt your feelings and you need to get over it, write a letter describing what you feel and how you feel. You will then be able to tell that person that you forgive them. Once you have written the letters, you have two choices. First, send the letter. This is if you feel it is appropriate. The second is to take the addressed letter, write it on the envelope and go outside to set it ablaze. As the letter catches fire, you will see that it is a sign that you have forgiven the sender and can now move on.

Chapter 8: Facing Reality

This kinda of madness has a special kind of pain. It's overwhelming when you're at your highest. Your ideas and feelings flow quickly, almost like shooting stars. They will keep you going until you find better and stronger ones. Shyness disappears. The right words and gestures suddenly appear, making it possible to capture others with your powerful words and gestures. There are things that interest even the most uninteresting of people. Sensuality and the desire for seduction are irresistible. You feel euphoria, ease, intensity, well-being financial omnipotence, financial well-being, financial power, and well-being. But this all changes. The rapid ideas are too fast, and the number of them is too high; confusion overtakes clarity. Memory disappears. Fear and concern replace the humor and absorption that used to be displayed on the faces of friends. Everything that used to move with grain is now against you. These were the caves you didn't even know existed. It will never be over, as madness creates its realities. - Kay Redfield Jamison

I am an optimist by nature and believe that all things happen the way they are meant to. However, this is true for me as well as my way of living and thinking. I don't expect you to believe or think like I do. I also don't intend to force anyone to be the same way. What would that do for you? It will only frustrate you, cause more stress, worsen your mood and trigger an episode that you don't need. I was recently told by someone that they don't enjoy hearing other people tell them how to adapt. They told me that they could feel any emotion they choose. Bipolar disorder sufferers, as well as any other person, should have the freedom to feel upset, sad or happy. Nobody wants to be told how to feel.

This chapter will help to you recognize that you have the right to feel what you want. One of my patients shared with me that they feel like a fox in the headlights when they're in a difficult situation. Panic and fear can make it hard for them to get out of a difficult situation. Then they will realize that they must deal with the situations they do not want to. I will not lie, it won't help. I'm also not in business of making others happy by sugarcoating situations. The journey you're about to embark on, in which you will learn how to manage emotions, is going be hard. You will be pulled out of your bubble, the place where you feel safe. According to me, people need to respect you, not see you a threat. They don't need star charts to make it seem like you have achieved a great milestone. Show them that you are the same person who was diagnosed with bipolar disorder before.

An Insider's Look at the Mind of Someone with Bipolar Disorder

When I look at my work as a writer, it's overwhelming. I have so much information running through my head. I need to reconsider how I present myself in order to not offend my audiences. It is crucial to give accurate information, and make sure I convey a reassuring tone so people feel that I understand their situation. I find it difficult to control my thoughts and there is so much I want. I constantly read what I have written. I may rewrite the paragraph several times before I am satisfied with how it turned out. I want my readers to stop reading at the end and stare in wonder before they start to implement the ideas I've shared.

I can only imagine how bipolar disorder patients might feel. My head may be full of information, but for those who are having manic episodes, their brains are spinning faster than anyone can imagine. I can't tell you what is going on inside someone with bipolar disorder. Individuals suffering from bipolar disorder or other mental disorders don't like sharing their feelings. They don't want people to notice them because of the stigmatism surrounding mental health issues. You may be interested in the bipolar episodes that see individuals with bipolar disorder dominate conversation and force the spotlight on them. Yes, it happens. But, that is their safety. It's important to remember that while we can see what happens, we cannot see their minds. It can be debilitating to witness a bipolar disorder sufferer's mind spin out of control.

Bipolar Disorders: The Chaos in their Minds

I have done extensive research by speaking with people and reading blogs from those living with bipolar disorder. My research is dependent on the individual and the situation. Everyone with bipolar disorder struggles with cohabitation with the thoughts in their heads. One of my interviewees said that the emotions they experience are related to makeup and paint color palettes. You can mix and match colors to create amazing masterpieces by looking at the color palettes. Individuals suffering from bipolar disorder will be able to see the colors, including reds, blues and greens. They will also see a variety of colors that when combined will make a mess. Because their emotions are high and overwhelming, they are unable see the potential. This makes it easy for them to feel overwhelmed and want to control their emotions.

I am sharing a few examples that may help others who don't have bipolar disorder to understand their loved ones and friends. Even those with bipolar disorder may find this list useful in helping others to understand what they're going through. The feeling of being in the middle of intense emotions and chaos can be akin to:

* Watching a boomerang reel in social media. A dog is running around trying to catch its tail.

* hold on tight to your heart so that it doesn't escape from your chest as you wait to see a dentist

* Drinking too many caffeinated energy drink or coffee.

* being trapped in a closed area with the sound a fly buzzing continuously, but it cannot see or escape capture

* one is at risk of losing a limb, while being afraid that an educator or

employer might be watching work in progress or monitoring the progress of tests.

It seems reasonable to assume that every person has had similar experiences as the ones in these examples at some point or another during their life. While many of these examples may frustrate us, most people will be able to adapt and continue with their daily tasks. Due to the short circuit in their brains, individuals with bipolar disorder don't have this "adapter" gene. The ability to feel anything can be multiplied 100 times to make them more emotional, which can cause manic or depressive episodes.

Learning how to recognize and observe triggers, emotions and thoughts that are tumultuous
This message goes out to everyone regardless of their mental health

condition. Everyone needs to be mindful of their surroundings. I don't know everything going on in you life, and you won't know what I'm going through. Many people do not know what their partner, best friend, or significant other think. Therapists and psychiatrists may agree to me that when I am dealing with a new patient, I need patience. I must establish that trust with them before they can believe that I only have positive intentions. This is how I help them cope. One strategy is to direct the thoughts that may threaten to enter the "episodes realm."

Did you ever feel so tired that the moment you touch your pillow, you instantly fall asleep? You do the usual routine of closing the door, setting an alarm, and filling the water bottle. You turn the lights off as you head to the bathroom to wash, brush, and use the toilet. You pull down the covers on your bed, remove the throw pillows and get into your bed. And then, just like that, you fall asleep. Before you know, your mind has been spinning since one thought after the next joined you at the slumber party. After what seems like a while, you look back at the time to see that it's now 3:30 a.m. Now you need to recalculate how many hours you can sleep before the alarm goes off.

Navigating Through the Storm of Thoughts

Although we may wish we could, we simply can't control how many thoughts come into our minds. Your thoughts will take over your head and make you feel like you're living rent-free. You do have control over intrusive thoughts. This is a common problem among humans everywhere. These thoughts become huge obstacles or boulders to you and make it difficult for you to find your way around. But guess what? These thoughts don't have to control the way that your mind makes you feel. We will work together to discover how to navigate around, between, and through those thoughts. I told you before that I wouldn't wear kid gloves for you. Do you believe this book will treat your bipolar disorder differently? Nah-ah! I want to help your be independent and make the most out of the unfortunate disorder that has entered your life.

We've established that thoughts are an integral part of our everyday lives. They don't need to be placed on a timetable or stopped popping up without permission. You have the option to choose how to deal with thoughts that come up. Some may address thoughts, while others might just ignore them. Then there are those who will pile on guilt, shame, embarrassment and shame for the thoughts. Did you think the thoughts came up? Because your thoughts are not controlled by you, it's impossible to stop them from coming into your head. These thoughts can be triggered by your own thoughts. Instead of dwelling on them, think about something else. I urge you to stop judging and blaming yourself for what you did not do. I can assure that your brain does not need the pressure associated with judging and analysing thoughts. To get through these thoughts it will take patience, self-control, and self-discipline. I believe you and know that you can do what I have done. Are you convinced of your own ability to do it?

Your Triggers
I needed to understand the origins of emotions and how they are learned. The information I have gathered has been varied. One of the articles I read was inspired by research by Professor

Joseph LeDoux of New York University as well Professor Richard Brown of City University of New York. Professors concluded that emotions do not come naturally to our brains. LeDoux and Brown 2017 stated that emotions are programmed in the brain by the looking, learning, recalling, and recalling of the emotions experienced. Another article stated that people are naturally emotional. Scott Trettenero authored the article for Psychreg online magazine.

You can go through the articles and try to understand them. However, emotions are something we experience every day. Learning how to recognize and organize your emotions and thoughts is the best way to manage them. Keep in mind that you don't control your emotions. You will need to practice to reach your goals. As you begin to learn how best to deal with emotions, it is important to be aware and mindful of your surroundings. It is said that Rome was not built in an hour, so slow and steady wins.

Aesop's The Hare and the Tortoise fable was one of the things that brought back fond memories. The arrogance of a hare meant that he believed he was unbeatable. The tortoise had a humble, kind, and nonjudgmental nature. The hare believed the race would be won and was invincible. Instead of racing to finish, he taunted and mocked his tortoise. His arrogance cost him victory because he couldn't believe the tortoise would reach the finish line due to his slow pace. Bipolar disorder patients are faced with a similar situation. But, it is happening in their heads. You are trying hard to prove yourself capable and fighting with yourself. Let me share one of my little secretes with you. Although I will not tell anyone about it, it is perfectly acceptable to be the tortoise. You can slow down and take time to get a better understanding of yourself.

Psychological and physical Triggers
Remember that no one knows your feelings better than you. You know exactly how you feel at any given moment. None of your caregivers or friends, nor medical professionals can tell whether you are experiencing this feeling or another, or if you are building up emotions that will send you spiraling.

* Do you feel that your emotions have gotten in the way of you and you aren't even aware?

* Have your missed or ignored signs that may indicate you are being triggered?

* Do your know how to identify potential triggers

Let's take you through a list that can indicate that there are psychological or other triggers that may be coming.

These signs are:
* A sudden feeling of fearfulness.

* A profound sense of sadness

* Feeling uncertain and insecure about a situation

* Feeling anxious or afraid in a situation

* Unexplained anger towards a situation which doesn't require emotions

* racing heart rate
* Feeling nauseated

* suddenly shaking and paling at thoughts of fearful situations

* Feelings like the world is spinning, but with vertigo.

* The ability to recall a traumatizing experience such as abuse

How to Recognize Your Emotional Triggers & Learn to Live With Them

Emotional triggers (also known as silent alarms) can affect many people. Individuals with bipolar disorder may have trouble dealing with them. This is where homework will be assigned. You will be able to identify the thoughts and emotions that consume your mind, how to let them go rent-free, as well as how to deal with emotional turmoil. This guide is designed to help you cohabitate effectively with those thoughts. It will also show you how to direct them towards their own boxes and not to the one they choose.

It is time to stand firm. When you experience any one, two,, or all of these triggers you have the right press the pause and take a step outside of the situation to observe what is going inside of your head. You may wish to keep your journal near you to record where you were at that particular moment. The act of noting everything can help you create a timeline. It will show you what you were doing at the time, what your thoughts were, and what feeling you had. It is possible to avoid future episodes by noting redundant details. Remember that emotions can relate to your mood. This list could go on and on, with emotions such as:

* Satisfied
* nostalgic
* angry
*
* Happy
* for love
* afraid
* tranquil

*

It is part of the exercise of taking an honest look at your emotions that you try to retrace those steps. You'll want to return back to the place you were mentally blocked from because it was too difficult. This is an important part your journey and for your mental health. This is not a cure-all. But it will help you identify and understand what triggers you. Understanding your triggers and the origins of your emotions will enable you to manage your mood episodes. This is a learning process and will require patience. However, I feel confident that you will succeed.

Another important reminder that I have mentioned before is that you shouldn't hide your emotions or thoughts. When you experience a trigger, you shouldn't hide or cover your head. Did you also know that you have the ability to be the Sherlock Holmes for your thoughts, emotions, and feelings? You are the best investigator you have because, as I said before, you know your self better than anyone. Ask yourself questions. Keep track of what you're learning by using your journal. It's best to confront your emotions and thoughts face-to-face, regardless of how strong the urge may be to ignore them. If you are unable to control your mood episodes, it is better to address them immediately.

The Art of Identifying Your Psychological and Physical Emotional Needs and Meeting These Needs

Your mental and bodily health is dependent on your willingness to help the body run its day-today activities. It's important to recognize that thoughts, emotions and feelings are not something we can ignore. Imagine a world where everyone walks around in a trance. Don't ignore your feelings, thoughts and emotions. Grab the bull by the nose, and you will be able to recognize and understand where your emotions come from.

This last section of the chapter is going help you think about and take into account your physical and mental needs. This is how your brain and body react to emotions. Let's take the opportunity to look at some examples that might help us identify and manage our emotions. This will ensure that we meet our psychological and physical needs. Use your journal to capture all of the experiences you have. A journal will help to organize a helpful guide for bipolar disorder individuals.

Hunger

Your psychological emotional need for food is to be satisfied. The body's natural response is to get food. The body will get a signal from its brain telling it it is hungry. Your body needs food in order to stay healthy. Your health may be compromised if your brain fails to send the messages it needs. Your brain will perceive this as your ignoring an emotion. When that happens you can feel physically impacted. Your body needs to be able to function. More importantly, food is essential for your brain to function properly. You don't want to feel the emotions that can trigger mood episodes. Create a schedule to remind your brain to eat three- to six times per day. Remember to also drink water.

Sufficient rest

This is a difficult subject for most people, regardless whether or not they have mental health issues. Everyone struggles with the subject of sleep. The psychological emotional need for sleep is paramount. Your body signals that it needs to be restful or take a break. After a hectic day of learning, working, and activity, sleep is essential to the body's healing process. Your brain must continue to make serotonin, so it can send happy messages out to the rest. Your brain must slow down to produce this neurotransmitter. Lack of enough sleep can cause mood swings that are hard to avoid. These great tips will help you ensure that you get the sleep that you need:

* Make sure you go to bed each night at the same times every night.
* Don't eat, drink or ingest anything within two to three hours of going to bed.
* Reduce consumption of caffeinated drinks and alcoholic beverages.
* Turn off your cell phones in your bedroom
* Get ready to stay in your bed all night.
* Avoid distractions and limit blue light device use.
* Use white noise to help you relax and feel peaceful.

This is something you should learn to adhere to. It may seem difficult to alter your habits but you know that it is important for your mental health. Sticking to a routine is the key to retraining your brain to sleep.

Calming the Eye of the Storm
You can feel what you want. You have control over your thoughts. You control both. All of it is yours, and no one else can take it without your permission. - Carlos Wallace
I have already mentioned that I will not treat your child with kid gloves. I presume that you have had enough of people treating yourself as fragile pieces of China porcelain. People will likely praise you for having an amazing day. People are likely watching you closely as you interact with customers or coworkers at work. The only safe place is the bathroom. This is where you can lock down the door and get five minutes of complete privacy. While people might be very well-meaning, they often don't fully understand what

it means that they should be watched, praised and treated like a broken winged bird. How much do I agree with my assumptions?

Everyone around will be waiting for your flight. Those same people are eager to give you advice on how to calm yourself and control your thoughts. Most people don't grasp the stress and anxiety that can come with such "helpful" advice. Your head will not roll off your head, you aren't fragile and your normal, imperfect self is fine. I have already said it, and I will again. Because you are your own person, you need to understand and accept that. Bipolar disorder can be diagnosed. Do you want the diagnosis to be made public in a "state of the nation" address? Do you want it to be declared in a state of the nation address? You don't have to be bothered by this kind of attention. You just want to live. People need to accept you just as you are. All you need is guidance in understanding and managing the little flaws that may exist in your central processing system.

Facing the Facts was the introduction. It was the beginning of our journey together. We looked at how to identify thoughts or emotions and how we can deal with things you can't change. Understanding them was key. Then you could face them, identify their source, handle them, and then lock them away in your mind's archive. It's a work-in-progress, but with lots of information and tips and tricks you can become a pro at helping yourself through difficult situations. You'll learn to be confident in your knowledge and how to recognize negative feelings and thoughts. I want to provide you with the information and give you the encouragement that you need in order to keep yourself three steps ahead if you are faced with any mood episodes.

It is possible to change negative thoughts and assumptions

Why not despise the negative nellies sneaking into your mind palace. They can place thoughts into your mind that relate directly to: you can't do this. You won't want the other. These negative nellies exist in everyone's head palace, regardless their mental health. They thrive on being in the heads of bipolar disorder patients because they know how to press the right buttons. They're on my radar, and it's time to let go of those negative nellies at your mind palace.

Now is the time to start your own covert task organization. This one-of a kind team is only made up of one person: you. With some basic knowledge and guidance, you'll be able build a stellar compound customized to your needs. Your compound will include compartments that allow for you to:

* A strategy room

* Separate all thoughts
* Participate in fact-finding tour
* immobilize negative energy - that includes negative nellies
* Learn how focus can be a challenge

When you are done with construction and have dealt with everything, you will be able identify and respond to your mood episodes. Your new compound will function as an early alarm system. It will notify you of potential triggers so you can avoid any mood episodes.

Adopting a strategy that works

Remember that this is about your autonomy and self-control. This is not about you, your spouse, partners, family, friends or colleagues. I want to put you in a transparent bubble. To show you what it's like to be alone with yourself and your thoughts without interference from well-meaning people. It can be very exhausting to be constantly under the spotlight, highlighting your bipolar disorder. Let's take a look below at various strategies to help change your negative thinking. Don't forget that these examples are flexible and can be adapted to meet your needs. You have the power to choose what works for you and your creativity is unlimited. I only offer chips and crumbs. The rest is up to the individual.

Take yourself out of the situation

I have spoken about this before and found it to be extremely effective. It is a technique I use with both my patients and my family. I believe it safe to say the world we live within is very diverse. You are just one of the seven million people who live in this universe. Everyone has their unique ideas and opinions about how things should work. Not everyone is satisfied with the way "their world" works. Not everyone gets along well with their neighbors, the community, and even their families. There are times when people disagree and argue. You cannot alter the way that others think or behave. One more thing: You cannot change the way others think and act. Here, I will give your "selfish" card to you and tell it that you must focus on yourself. Your mental wellbeing is more important than fixing another's income loss or break-up.

To be able to see the positive in a situation, you must be able take a step back. This should be something that you do from the very first moment you are exposed or given negative energy. The new perspective will help you see the problem. Seek out the perspective of other participants and match it with yours. What if you could reach an amicable settlement without getting all heated? Can you see what others are trying to convey? It is important to keep calm and practice a simple breathing technique to help regulate your heartbeat. It is important to remember that the pain you feel from a bipolar episode can last forever. Remember to pay attention to your brain and that your bipolar disorder can be managed with ease.

Turning Negatives Into Positives

This section requires your participation. I want to offer you some tips on how to transform negative thoughts into constructive actions. Don't let anyone tell your feelings. Make a few lists with your pen and journal. Let me show you some exercises to help you get rid of negative thoughts. If you are not able to use any of the above exercises, please send them in to the mind palace archives. You will not lose sleep worrying about something you cannot control. And it may not all work as you expect. It's all okay!

* Make lists that highlight your strengths. Write down positive compliments.

* Ask friends and family for help in identifying your strengths.

* The more confident that you are, the more you should continue adding to your checklists.

* Make posters from your lists and put them up where you can easily see them each day, or multiple times per week.

* Never forget that you are strong, and that your greatest friend is you.

Restructuring what you are thinking about can help you turn your negative thoughts around and transform them into something good. You could simplify negative thoughts by breaking them apart and categorizing them according you needs or where they play in your daily life. Keep what you have, and what you don't need. You should always be aware of your feelings. Don't be afraid to be selfish about your time, energy and thoughts.

Your Bipolar Mind: The Enemy

Human beings make the worst enemies. While mental health is important, we can all agree that people have a tendency to judge other people. I have met many people that have said they don't judge because everyone deserves fairness. That is until you see someone in a room covered in tattoos, with more piercings than anyone has ever seen and with tie-dyed hair. The moment is witnessed by many who experience the sight, their jaws drop to the floor, their eyes are bigger than saucers and they begin mental gymnastics.

I am trying make the point that, while people "normally" say something, their actions or reactions are quite different. The reactions of others can have a significant impact on a person suffering from bipolar disorder. You might visit a restaurant to meet someone you know for lunch. You walk into the restaurant and suddenly feel as if everyone is watching your every move as you make it over to your friend. You start to feel self-conscious. Your heart rate starts to speed up. Your palms feel sweaty. Your mind is constantly working overtime and you can sense that you are getting ready for a massive panic attack. The smile of your friend is a sign that you are smiling. You then look around the restaurant and notice that no one is actually looking at you. You entered the restaurant thinking everyone was staring at me. You assumed these people knew about your private information.

You can stop using panic paddles

Be careful not to grab the bull's nose ring and run. Stop allowing negative thoughts to take root in your head. I'm trying help you to create a calm and peaceful environment that will prevent depression and manic episodes. The best way for me to help you is to stop you from being overwhelmed by assumptions. Let's try one of those tools we mentioned in the previous section: to take yourself out of the situation. Take a step back. Try looking at it from an outsider's point of view. Ask yourself a few questions like:

* Why do people think they are focusing all their attention on me?

* Why shouldn't I believe this scenario is possible?

* Am I able to see the dangers?

* Have I been properly dressed?

Be truthful in your assessment of the situation. You don't have to lie about the situation. You're the one responsible for assessing your thoughts and trying to figure out where they came from.

* How did you arrive to these assumptions?

* Why are these assumptions important to you?

* Does your gut feel like it is playing tricks on me or are there serious concerns?

Never be afraid asking questions. I believe you can never ask for too many questions. Many people can be a do now and then type of person. But for someone who has mental health concerns it is important to keep their eyes on what is happening in their heads. You might just discover that you are being sensitive, and no one is judging or talking about you.

The panic paddles might be a temporary remedy for a long-term, or ongoing problem. I use the phrase "problem" because everyone finds a way to make someone feel better when they are feeling uneasy. Individuals suffering from bipolar disorder have different problems. I don't want to provide a solution for people who come to see me for therapy. I warned you, this book won't have kid gloves. You'll get compassion, understanding as well as self-help strategies and exercises.

The Contingency Plan will help you to avoid triggers

Triggers can be hard to avoid. They will creep up without you realizing. A manic episode is when you suddenly feel overwhelmed and you can feel perfectly fine. There are many ways you can reduce the emotion and feelings that accompany triggers. All the advice I have shared can be modified to meet your needs. I mentioned in the past that what works one way may not work another. Therefore, I offer you options and choices.

Many people have spoken out about how to identify potential triggers, analyze and pair thoughts and emotions with your feelings and assess situations that can cause anxiety or stress. I am here to help you devise a plan for contingency that will help manage your triggers when they arise. This plan might help you stay ahead. It will require practice and the ability to modify old habits or eliminate them completely to build new ones that can most likely enhance your quality-of-life. This contingency will help those with bipolar disorder manage anxiety disorders and minimize their risk.

Avoid distracting yourself from important things

You don't have the right to overwhelm your brain by thoughts and information that may be damaging to your mental (and/or physical) health. This could include spending less time on mobile devices, playing games, and absorbing negative information via social media platforms. Scheduling your screen time is important. You must also adhere to the rules you create. Distractions occur daily. Some distractions are impossible to avoid, like the neighbor's cat running onto your roof or the branches falling on your roof in middle of a storm.

Regular breaks

I found that writers need to take breaks throughout the day. This helps me focus and keep my mind clear. It is not easy to focus for long periods of a task. It is easy for our brains to get tired. This is when we lose sight of what we are doing. You may have experienced this yourself. After spending hours working on something, you realize you haven't accomplished what you wanted. You reach for the panic pedals to escape from the situation because your thoughts boxes are starting to open, and are threatening the chaos. One example of what you could do during a short break is:

* Stop what are you doing.
* Stand up.
* Enjoy a glass water or any other beverage.
* Focus your attention on the objects in front of you.
* Make a loop around the garden.

A ten minute break is a great way to clear the fog and refocus your focus, which will help boost productivity. There are many other things you could include in your contingency plan.

* Choose one activity to focus on at a particular time.
* Get enough sleeping.
* Always be mindful of your health.
* Stay focused on today. You can't change yesterday. Tomorrow has yet to arrive.
* You can listen to calming music to calm the soul.

www.ingramcontent.com/pod-product-compliance
Lightning Source LLC
Chambersburg PA
CBHW060500030426
42337CB00015B/1666